First published by AuthorHouse 8/23/2005

Second Edition: 8/7/2008

ISBN: 1-4184-2374-2 (sc)
ISBN: 1-4208-4527-6 (dj)

Library of Congress Control Number: 2005900587

Printed in the United States of America
Bloomington, Indiana

This book is printed on acid-fee paper.

D1502600

ACTION HAS NO SEASON

STRATEGIES AND SECRETS
TO GAINING
WEALTH AND AUTHORITY

BY MICHAEL V. ROBERTS, J.D.

authorhouse"

1663 Liberty Drive, Suite 200
Bloomington, Indiana 47403
(800) 839-8640
www.AuthorHouse.com

FORWARD

So why did I write this book? I wrote this book for my four children: Michael Jr., Jeanne, Fallon, and Meaghan. After having built a reasonable amount of wealth, I watched my offspring leave for college and law school with hopes of fulfilling their matriculation goals. Once they left for college, I realized that advanced degrees were not enough. In order to ensure their success in this ever-changing global business world, they would need the advice and counsel of a visionary capitalist such as me.

This book will give them a level of guidance that was not taught in school. These hard-core realities are seldom discussed, but they are always on stage in the real world.

These are the secrets of success. It all starts with becoming more enlightened. I adore wisdom and deplore ignorance. Ignorance produces constant failure in businesses. I love to observe uncommon progress and miraculous successes through the utilization of wisdom. It invigorates me to observe those people whom I lecture reach for the key of wisdom and unlock the door of exceptional success in their lives.

A very small key will unlock the door to enormous riches. Small changes in your life can create great futures. There are laws and principles that govern one's life. Discovering those laws can instantly and radically change the course of your business and life.

During my college and law school years, I read some powerful books that discussed the possible results of Action and existentialism when implemented in a person's life. After applying my interpretation to these readings, I began to live and breathe these concepts, which lead to the increase of my energy and vigor. The result was the formation of a powerful force that enabled me to compel my future into existence.

If you allow yourself to recognize this powerful, undiscovered secret of life, you will realize that this revelation has always been inside of you. It's your inner voice calling for Action.

Nevertheless, did I really know how to respond to it?

I was always a sharp-eyed, vigilant person. I read and dissected everyone close to me. I paid attention to every business discussion with complete focus, but that declamatory question persisted. What was this inner voice saying and how should I act upon it?

After several years of executing business deals in the traditional method of submitting well-written business plans, I still did not listen to my inner voice or my instincts that were diverting me to a different plan of Action.

I discovered it! I instantly understood the importance of Action combined with wisdom. I knew why the successful were flourishing. I understood why people around me were failing. I also knew the mindset of the conquering and exceptionally triumphant businessperson.

As I reviewed my experiences in business and life, I determined that:

- **An Experience recognized becomes celebrated**
- **An Experience celebrated becomes rewarded**
- **An Experience rewarded eventually lives throughout your life**.

The lessons and philosophy in this book are the highly sought after, missing links to a meaningful existence. It will center your focus and create magnetism around you. It will cause those people in strategic places to pursue you professionally and personally as they continue to grow and develop.

You are the architect of your life. You are the inventor of your destiny. Just as Michelangelo could take a piece of stone, chip away the non-essential pieces and produce "David", you too can chip away the status quo traditions attempting to restrict you from achieving, and manifest your vision into your destiny through Action.

Sharing this information will guide you in the direction of momentous success. This book will motivate you to change from a life of hardship to one of affluence. It will answer the questions masked within you, while unleashing more enthusiasm than you have ever known!

I pass on this legacy to my children and to the future leaders of humankind. I offer them the keys to unlock the hidden potential that is within all seekers of wealth and authority.

It is now in your hands!

Take Action!

The possibilities are endless!

I wrote this book for you.

Michael V. Roberts

TABLE OF CONTENTS

Forward   v

Preface   xiii

Acknowledgements   xvii

Introduction   xxi

Chapter 1
    Commencing Action   1
Chapter 2
    Shape Your Vision   9
Chapter 3
    Work Fosters Growth   13
Chapter 4
    The Picture of Self   19
Chapter 5
    Follow Your Calling   25
Chapter 6
    Your Focal Point   41
Chapter 7
    Genetic Code: Flesh vs Mind   49
Chapter 8
    Avoid the Utilitarian Life   55
Chapter 9
    The Paradox   59
Chapter 10
    Mastering Your Emotions   65
Chapter 11
    Summon Your Motivation   69

Chapter 12
      Your Inner Constitution   73
Chapter 13
      Natural Rhythms   77
Chapter 14
      Leadership and Vision   91
Chapter 15
      Breaking Barriers   97
Chapter 16
      Transacting Business   105
Chapter 17
      Final Thoughts   115

Reader Commentary & Book Reviews   125

About The Author   139

Appendix

News Articles:

"A Legacy of Honoring Entrepreneurial Excellence",
Ernst & Young Magazine, November 2007   153

"Fake It Till You Make It", Forbes Magazine,
October 16, 2000   158

"Roberts Brothers Oversee Growing
$460 Million 34-Company Empire",
St. Louis Commerce Magazine, May, 2003   161

"The Kings of Kingshighway",
Riverfront Times, March 17-23, 2004   171

"Mike Roberts is a capitalist for his time",
St. Louis Post Dispatch, June 25, 2004   189

"B.E. 100s", <u>Black Enterprise Magazine</u>,
2007   193

"The Roberts Brothers", <u>Missouri Meetings &</u>
<u>Events,</u> Spring 2006   195

"Brothers Who Art Thou", <u>St. Louis Magazine</u>,
Spring 2006   203

SPEECHES   215

"The Greatest Time in History to be in Business", Speech to Black Advertising and Marketing Professionals, September 21, 1995

"The Shaping of Black Entrepreneurship in the Next Millennium…the 21st Century Awaits You", Morehouse College Executive Lecture Series, October 29, 1997

PREFACE

"There are always opportunities through which businessmen can profit handsomely if they will only recognize and seize them."

-J. Paul Getty

Nobility is not a birthright, and character is not inherited. It's only your Action that builds the true self inside. There are no perfect men or women in this world, only perfect intentions. Perfection, however, can be approached when you take Action. Action rests on the belief that:

What cannot be explained must be tolerated.
Fear cannot exist when happiness subsists.
Loneliness cannot survive where confidence resides.
Sadness cannot stay alive when joy thrives.

Action solves the challenges of life and implements the tools to fulfill dreams.

PROBLEMS are intricate, unsettled beliefs. Problems are viewed as mistakes and become obstacles in one's life. One's outlook or perspective enables one to surpass these seeming problems. If you change defeatist thoughts into optimistic thoughts, then you will release the problems and find a victorious solution.

SPIRITUAL BELIEFS are the incorporeal thoughts of man. These spiritual thoughts enrich society. Winning occurs when your performance reflects your higher spiritual views. This inner spirituality must balance and connect with your outward existence to provide an unfettered field of endless solutions. It is these solutions that represent your purpose or calling.

SOLUTIONS are answers and explanations to troubled circumstances. A state of continuity can occur only when you choose to think and act out of your higher spiritual self. This Action enables you to meet your objectives.

Action accomplishes a lifestyle of admiration, contentment, and authenticity. To achieve wealth and authority, one must stay in control of their self-esteem and commitment to enjoy their existence.

This book offers the tools and skill sets to empower you with the realization, discernment, intellectual capacity and philosophy needed when facing the challenges of the business and political world. Adversity, deprivation, and distractions are common obstacles in one's life.

My book is brought to life on the front and back covers by the unique talents of Sam Lawson, Creative Director, Roberts Broadcasting Company.

Front cover photo by Michael Gregory of Imperial Imagery with Michael V. Roberts, Jr. as technical director.

To all of you, I will be forever grateful.

INTRODUCTION

UNDERSTAND YOUR ERA

In the year 2001, mankind embraced a new century. Many people are caught in the traditions of the past, while others are transitioning with new insights, sensitivities, and visions. Successful individuals tend to have a historical perspective and can sense a historical convergence in society's way of life. New methods of making fortunes are in the air. It is everywhere. The 20th century introduced us to an Industrial Society that created history-making inventions, which shape today's world.

If we look down the corridor of time at the significant milestones of modern man, we can measure a progressive growth in the methods of communication. This past century exploded in areas of telecommunication, broadcasting, computer technology, medicine, space science, transportation, education, telephony, and green energy alternatives. We are now living in a global society.

A short assessment reveals and defines a global paradigm shift that has changed our lives forever. The elimination of the Cold War and the emergence of international terrorism, global capitalism and economic interdependence, a robust international banking and stock market, and the Internet confirm the dominance of a global economy.

Everyday is a race for people of Action. The successful entrepreneur is sprinting towards the fulfillment of their dreams. To compete in this race, you must not only have teammates, but you must learn to pass the baton to the next runner. If the baton is dropped or not cleanly passed, time will be lost, and your race will be over regardless of the first runner's speed. The track coach may use a stopwatch in determining the speed of the team, but in business, you determine your success by other measurements.

Achieving success requires flexibility by you and your associates. Historically, you were required to "stay the course," but today, your course may undergo dramatic alterations with clear diversions and transformations from your original business plan or vision.

The Actionaire

People of Action or as I have coined them "Actionaires" understand that their measurement of success is based on thoughts and criteria never believed or conceived five years ago. In the fast paced information age, one must be very cautious in protecting the "status quo".

The status quo is relative, not progressive. The status quo is the traditional method of society. Every aspect of society has a status quo or tradition. Your beliefs in business methods and product creation are almost certain to change as you mature and progress in your endeavors. We must not be overly dogmatic with our beliefs. Avoid the trap of insisting that the status quo be retained. Protecting the status quo means never "rock the boat," "stay the course," and do everything as it has always been done.

In actuality, those viewpoints of protecting the status quo are based entirely on limited growth and inadequate knowledge. The fear of change ultimately drives those viewpoints. The Actionaire comprehends the importance of standardizing beliefs and traditions. Traditions that are effective and consistent with your era are fine. When your traditions and beliefs lose their beneficial nature, you should abandon them.

The Actionaire understands the fundamentals of traditions. As maturity increases, the Actionaire learns that their incorrect assessment of right and wrong often results from limited contact, exposure, knowledge, education, opportunities, and counsel.

Entrepreneurial Actionaires will make changes when a methodology is no longer effective. Actionaires have vision and can spot obsolescence. Style and design in fashion distinguish each succeeding generation. This rule of changing with the present should apply in all businesses. Many leaders, who presently govern the affairs of companies, are no longer effective. They fail to transform to the nuances and desires of the present generation. They try to fly a jet with the skills and traditions of a propeller pilot. They try to attract the hip-hop music audiences with music by Perry Como, Johnny Mathis, or the Beach Boys. Actionaire business executives have the power and wisdom to win a generation that is newly defining purpose and style. Those executives who fail to respond to change, may call themselves leaders, but they are nothing more than managers who pathetically sustain the status quo.

The Actionaire is always prepared to change. Frequently, present day leaders lack the ability to relate to their constituency. Our society now operates in a global telecommunications environment. A great awakening is happening around the world. This new global connection will make business more competitive and diverse. The rate of speed inside this new environment will create exponential business growth. The successful entrepreneur will not be a slow paced gatekeeper or a status quo disciple. The traditional managers are frequently over powered and rendered persona-non-gratis by the dominant Actionaire.

Victorious people, in business and in all other walks of life, are **Actionaires**.

Chapter 1

COMMENCING ACTION

Nothing is as formidable as taking Action; authority and wealth are only achieved through Action.

In order to develop your talents and skills to reach your capacity and fulfill your aptitude, you must become an Actionaire. Your life will be transformed by recognizing the need to undertake Action. Action is natural to human existence and pertinent to our growth process. All life is in a state of Action and nothing can prevent it from evolving. The principle of creation underscores the human existence and the importance of Action.

The renowned statement, Action speaks louder than words, contains a conviction that will bring tremendous strength, truth, and intensity to your life. If you understand the inescapable truth that nothing remains the same and change is constant, you will minimize your failures and maximize your success by becoming an Actionaire with every endeavor.

Another frequently used statement suggests that there are three types of Action within our existence: that which happens to you; that which happens around you; and that which you make happen. One of the great tragedies in our society is that less than one percent of our population takes Action effectively. This concept is evidenced by one generally accepted statistic: less than one percent of the world's population holds ninety-nine percent of the wealth.

Most people are victims of another person acting upon their ideas, visions, or created opportunities. When this inaction occurs, it often results in frustration, depression and hostility. Actionaires have little time to experience these roller coaster type emotions of instability. They are too busy manifesting their dreams or seeking out new deals. These opportunities are found both in local or familiar settings and from remote locations.

Opportunities will arise from the most unexpected corners. It takes Action to manifest them.

Pioneering new and bold ventures is the behavior of an Actionaire. When faced with a failure, a company downturn, a personal catastrophe, or any negative challenge, Actionaires always strive to alter or redirect those tribulations into positive energy; thereby, formulating an enviable outcome.

If you are teetering at the threshold of Action and feel trepidation in regard to changing your current direction or career, you must enhance your confidence and embrace change by pursuing your desires and inner calling. This self-motivation will best occur through taking Action with a positive mindset and adhering to the message of this book. Deciding on how to execute Action will catapult you into fulfilling your calling. Once you boldly embrace Action, you will stimulate, activate, and release the force of your possibilities. At this point, you will discover your purpose in life, acquire authority, and amass wealth.

Living humans should necessitate Action throughout their

Action that advances creation. The true Actionaire is working or building if not he or she is obsolete.

If you enjoy what you are doing, you never work a day in your life.

Chapter 4

THE PICTURE OF SELF

The Actionaire is an audacious doer on a quest for personal attainment. They are unlike the individual who fails to ameliorate their life situation because of a negative self-image. An unfavorable self-image characterized by thoughts of doubt, incompetence, and pessimism engenders a feeling of personal dissatisfaction. This disagreeable self-image prohibits an individual from accomplishing the goals that are important in life and successful careers.

An Actionaire is free of codependency and addictions, and has a positive self-image and self-appreciation. Their attitude supports personal achievement. In contrast, many underachieving individuals have a self-deprecating attitude that dominates their total being and exterminates their motivation for personal achievement. This self loathing individual abrogates their own battle of acquiring the best in their life. The Actionaire creates the time to develop and maintain a favorable self-impression. With this attitude, they have the ability to succeed and the capacity for personal enrichment. Actionaires have skills and techniques that enable them to create success in their personal and business life. These valuable tools are rooted in their self-esteem. One's confidence and satisfaction with self establishes a positive self-image. Every aspect of achievement emerges from an emotionally secure, fully functional person of high self-esteem. Having a positive self-view is basic to obtaining emotional security and the ability to be a functional person.

What is the true essence of self-esteem? The Actionaire perceives it as an adequate and confident impression of self, fueled by a positive attitude, high self-expectations, and high self-appreciation. In the Actionaire's mind, high self-esteem acts as a catalyst in attaining a peace of mind and personal achievement. High, positive self-esteem is crucial and essential to becoming an Actionaire.

Although everyone wants and needs it, many individuals fall short. They seem to be forbidden from possessing higher levels of self-esteem. What is it that alienates them from self-love at all times?

When your self-esteem is positive, you will become more optimistic, and life will in turn offer you more opportunities. The Actionaire has an abundance of self-love and truly appreciates every moment of their existence. The Actionaire feels safe and personally empowered. They embody the courage to face new challenges and explore foreign areas in their widely expanding life. Their life experiences are embellished with texture, taste, zest, and flavor. Through the energy generated by their self-appreciation, the power of personal attainment becomes enormous.

On the other hand, those people who are diffident and

insecure tend to aspire to mediocrity. They support the status quo and adhere to the philosophy of "never rock the boat." These individuals seem to operate on keeping their own illumination from glowing. Frequently, they are shy and easily embarrassed. In efforts to develop favorable impressions, they may try to attain success through mere "will power." Pure "will power" will not create a complimentary, constructive or objective impression of you. "Will power" alone is an immense effort and should not influence all your experiences in life or career. Regularly, individuals enter the business world with an idea and strong "will power." They have the desire, but little vision and a weak self-esteem. Failure follows the entrant because they do not have the "know how" to succeed. They do not have the essentials of self-esteem.

Remember, low or high self-esteem is based on your own self-image and not how you are attempting to have other people perceive you. It is how you feel about yourself, not how you appear to be. If you can change your initial thoughts about yourself, then you can change your representation or image of yourself. In turn one can change their self-esteem.

This philosophy is the "know how." Your self-view or personal perception determines your appearance to the rest of the world. It is this picture of self that shapes a new self-appreciation. With a positive self-image, your life and business will find success in every new challenge. You must create positive inner thoughts to support courageous behavior. One must change any negative pervasive thought and aggressively strive to increase self-esteem. These new thoughts will lead to independence, self-reliance, and personal inner wealth. Without it, you are apprehensive, hesitant, angst-redden, and destined for failure.

The Actionaire develops a personal picture of self while creating a depiction for others. As you study these pictures, one will soon discover another image beginning to take shape. The Actionaire sees self not as what he/she has been, but as what he/she is going to be. For you, self-confidence reveals a picture of - not where you have been - but where you are heading. Your self-esteem does not view a picture of your past deeds. Instead, it witnesses a picture of your future Actions. It is the vision you follow. A fresh mental picture of yourself sets your goal.

Individuals who do not follow the Actionaire beliefs cannot achieve their destiny because they continue to reinforce their picture of self as a failure; therefore, they permit the self-definition of being foolish, imprudent, or obtuse to overpower them. In its place, they must see a self that is mentally sharp, brilliant, and a winner. See yourself as a success and you will become a success. Like a photo, you can clear up your self-esteem after it has been faded or blemished. You can always reshape your self-image by bringing out your fervent points, strong qualities, and

positive features. It is a mistake to live with a distorted picture of self. The picture you develop of yourself is crucial to your success or failure.

Regardless of their circumstances, Actionaires will always feel positive about their Actions. They will succeed because they have the flexibility and skill to change a negative self-image. It is by their choice that the Actionaire can change their inner representations irrespective of their circumstances to feel positive about self. They are protected by this ability to change, which allows them to raise their level of self-esteem on the spot. Their emotions deeply affect the structuring of their life and business. These emotions provide important information about how they make personal pronouncements or fashion company strategies. The Actionaire interprets their emotional behavior, takes the appropriate Action to change their thinking, and in turn change the picture of their self.

When making a business decision, the Actionaire considers their emotion-based information seriously. However, once recognized and evaluated in the context of the opportunity, the Actionaire will use both their emotional and learned analyzes to formulate a sound stratagem of positive Action.

Chapter 5

FOLLOW YOUR CALLING; CREATE YOUR DESTINY

Each of us is extraordinary and distinctive. There is a brilliant uniqueness in each person on earth. Our appearance, aura, and energy may be similar or we may literally be indistinguishable twins, however, no two people are absolutely identical. Nature has created this inimitability that makes the various components of our bodies equal, but different. Only you possess your individual personality, talents, skills, and ideas. Only you contain your exact DNA or heredity. Each of us is here for a specific reason, purpose or calling. This realization proposes two questions. Why are you here, and what is your destiny?

You have a unique design and function that will authorize you to fulfill your destiny. We, individually, have a calling that is special and personal. No person can substitute for you. Your calling cannot be taken or performed by anyone else. It is tailored to you, and may be varied and diverse. When one has numerous callings, one must realize that a wide-ranging series of Actions and activities will flow with life.

All life starts and finishes with your contribution to the functionality of society. This contribution to the ethos of society is the creator of the destination for your life's journey. It is the object that one wills or resolves to have. It is the aspiration for the inspiration to take Action. Until you unveil your calling, existence has little meaning. A person can only attain true fulfillment when performing their calling. Fulfilling your potential is the ultimate definition of success. Your calling is an integral part of you, and your entire life's satisfaction is only possible if you, personally, complete your destiny.

The Actionaire endeavors to be who they were born to be. Their vision is clear and their self-esteem is positive; therefore, their confidence and judgment are intact. They fully entrust in their calling. Being fully operative in these variables is necessary to achieve their goals. The Actionaire will confront many obstacles that must be overcome to reach their overall life's purpose. The Actionaire knows what they want to establish and understands that achieving it may vary. Their vision of purpose combats the many plots and schemes that others may place before them to prevent their success. All experiences in the life of an Actionaire are intricately and perfectly related, which are ultimately linked to their calling.

The universe, the world, and society have a purpose larger than your specific end. Your calling is fulfilled when your individual Action is exemplified within its arena. In a society, one person's purpose must aid another in fulfilling their purpose. Nothing, therefore, exists for itself alone. Nature and humanity subsist for each other and their own species within their communal environment. Every person in society exists for each other. An isolationist or loner cannot fulfill their calling without the works of others. All life forms survive and live for each other.

The greatest travesty in life is failing to follow your calling. People who fail to search for or fulfill their known calling live without ever understanding the reason of their existence. Their existences are actually dangerous because they live lives that are full of frustrations and regrets. Until you understand yourself and create a positive picture of yourself, you are not truly in control of yourself.

Often, an individual spends hours and days that turn into months and years trying to figure out what to do with their life. They devise vague or fruitless goals. They express their desire to live in a larger house, drive an expensive car, and acquire the life of the rich and famous. They always fall short in gaining these material things. They fail because they wrongly focus upon these seemingly right ideals. Every person is adroit and magnificent in his or her own right. We must awaken these hidden skills and the brilliance within us to uncover our destiny. We must zealously follow our personal callings.

The Actionaire avidly pursues their unique calling, aspirations, and dreams. They ascertain a sense of importance and application to their purpose. There is a craving for relevant Action. The Actionaire has an internal motivation that drives behavior towards the control of their environment. They are elevated to higher goals through a sense of self-esteem, self-appreciation, self-expression, and passion to follow their calling.

Each encountered hindrance is used as a learning tool to achieve the possibilities within them. The trail to success will have bumps and detours, but eventually, it will come to the desired end. If the Actionaire made a decision that interfered with their calling, they make arrangements to reform their Actions to move off the detour.

They use this experience to refine their approach. With their calling back in focus, the Actionaire transforms a mistake into corrective Action.

The Actionaire is not stalled by the past. Their calling remains true no matter which path they take or past mistakes they have made. The Actionaire remains focused on achieving the intended goal. Nothing can cancel your calling. The society in which we live is waiting for you to fulfill your calling. We are part of a universal purpose. Each of us has a responsibility to complete our calling. When this universal purpose is not achieved, society fails. Today, many people have lost sight of society's collective calling. No person is outside of this calling. It is imperative that people remain cognizant of their obligation to society. Understanding and pursuing this worldwide calling is vital, especially when life becomes meaningless.

The capitalist Actionaire seizes business opportunities as they are presented or invented. They face these new and challenging ventures with courage, a reasonable knowledge of the subject matter and a vision of the outcome.

Regardless of your origin, or station in life, there is a demand for your purpose. Your residency does not govern your calling. Life presents unique opportunities that all Actionaires must capture. This calling is your destiny. The Actionaire creates their destiny. They do not wait for destiny to come to them. You must take Action to create your destiny; life is not a rehearsal. Life is like a fine musical instrument. The sounds of music you create depend on how you play it. The Actionaire plays life everyday as if tomorrow does not exist.

What is destiny?

> **Destiny is invented, accept it.**
> **Destiny is education, learn it.**
> **Destiny is a song, croon it.**
> **Destiny is an enigma, assemble it.**
> **Destiny is a venture, invest in it.**
> **Destiny is a sport, play it.**
> **Destiny is opportunity, engage it.**
> **Destiny is a challenge, experience it.**
> **Destiny is a mission, act upon it.**
> **Destiny is a mystery, solve it.**
> **Destiny is poignant, face it.**
> **Destiny is the goal, achieve it.**

A PERSONAL ANECDOTE:

Seizing the opportunity......

During one of the first few months after my brother, Steven and I were in our first offices in downtown St. Louis when a young lawyer, who shared the adjacent suite, stopped us in the hallway. I didn't know at the time, that what he was asking me would indescribably change the direction of our business and help clarify one of my callings.

He was a liaison to a broadcast consultant who was seeking a St. Louis based minority businessman, preferably an African American, with an interest in pursuing a television station license.

When asked if I was interested I took the standard Actionaire response. "YES, OF COURSE." With little else but the consultant's telephone number I took Action and made the call. Shortly thereafter my brother and I invited him in our offices.

This consultant advised us of the procedures for pursuing a Federal Communications Commission's (FCC) broadcast license. He added to that discussion the proposed costs attributed to this process. There was a need for an FCC law firm based in Washington D.C., a professional broadcast engineering firm and the consultant to guide us through the process.

The timing was good for us because we fortunately had just been awarded a large business management-consulting contract providing us with just enough money to risk the labors of seeking a TV station license.

We were advised that the licensing "process" amounted to the FCC deciding on the best applicant. The applicant considerations included but were not limited to: who would best represent the local community with this public trust; will there be a integration of ownership into the operations of the station; what is the communications background of the applicant; what is the evidence of financial capability; submittal of an accurate engineering report; and, demonstrating a special characteristic of the applicant that would grant preferential treatment by the FCC policies, to wit, belong to a racial minority group.

Our company's team scored well in each of these categories. Steve and I presented ourselves strongly as local representatives; considering we were both elected officials and graduates of St. Louis law schools. I had a college degree in communications arts, with courses in broadcasting and Steve worked at his college radio station. We identified and acquired site control for the broadcast tower allowing for the engineering to be submitted without questions.

The final positive was that we were minority applicants at a time when the FCC was expressing a desire to diversify its ownership in broadcast licensing. This was to be our guarantee to success until others followed our application and filed for the same license. Five other groups applied after us, all of whom represented themselves as a minority applicant.

Now the battle field shifted and it became a true fight over which was the best team. The FCC on a comparative and competitive basis studied this question.

Pursuing this quest was now becoming time consuming and very expensive. The opponents were out to win at any cost. Losing was not an option for us.

We attacked these competitors on every available issue. With some there were flaws in their engineering. One group copied our engineering and tried to pass if off as their own. They might have been successful except they copied certain longitude and latitude coordinates incorrectly. This was a real-life example that in business you can eliminate your opponents on pure stupidity.

Others were disqualified for technical reasons; and, to achieve ultimate victory we eliminated some the old fashion way, we bought them off.

Not withstanding the fact that the FCC ruled to award the license to the Roberts Broadcasting Company, we had one group to appeal that decision driving us into years of legal appeals and substantial unnecessary expenses. Despite the sour grape mentality of those opponents, we prevailed.

In 1989 we launched our first TV station, eight years after we began the application process. It was the newest broadcast station in the St. Louis market in twenty years.

Over time we grew our TV broadcast business e exponentially. At one time we owned television stations in the following markets Denver CO, Nashville TN, Salt Lake City UT, Raleigh Durham NC, Hartford CT, Albuquerque NM, Santa Fe NM, Mobile AL, Jackson MS, and Columbia SC.

During the life of these business ventures, we have engaged a wide range of activities. As the times changed we have privately held, sold and taken some of our stations to the public market. This is an excellent example of never giving up your vision and understanding that only with Action can you win. Surrounding each of the acquisitions are interesting learning experiences for you the reader. However, that is information for a future book.

Knowledge, Opportunity & Vision........

As mentioned, we did make decisions to sell and merge some of our TV stations. Why? In the mid 1990's the FCC issued a notice announcing it was placing telecommunication spectrum on the market for bid. My research revealed this spectrum would be used for digital telephone services, known as Personal Communication Services (PCS).

Philosophically, I wanted my company to be absorbed in the emerging "Information Age." This Age was rapidly taking its place in history, exactly as the Agricultural Age and the Industrial Age. Actionaires of those times succeeded in amassing great wealth because they had the vision and the courage to take Action as the current changed.

I envisioned this emerging Information Age as the opportunity of my time. Owning TV stations was my first effort to plant my stake on the Information Highway.

The die was cast for me when the FCC mandated all television full power television station licensees to begin converting, from the time tested and comfortable analogue signal, to digital. I was one of the few in the traditional broadcast industry who understood the potential use of the digital application. The vision of this digital future inspired me to begin making plans to capitalize on what I knew was coming next.

As an owner of bandwidth, soon to carry us into a new world of greater video clarity, I predicted, these digital signals would lead the way to indefinite future opportunities. The early stages of change would include interactive communications with your TV sets and the Internet.

The Actionaire would conclude this change would offer possibilities for unique or opportunistic ventures. In turn, it would advance one's businesses, providing accretive growth in times to come.

When placed in the path of this emerging business, what becomes the most valuable commodity to own? It is spectrum, which will serve as the wireless backbone for these promising undertakings.

When the FCC announced their intention to auction the PCS spectrum for new wireless digital telephones, I knew my company needed to be in this hunt. After making certain my businesses were ready to enter the playing field; we joined the bidding war for FCC PCS "C" Block licenses.

The FCC established six licensing categories. These categories consisted of three bidding blocks: A, B and C, were for 30 megahertz; and, another three: D, E and F, were blocks for 10 megahertz of power. Blocks C and F were set aside for limited bidding by Designated Entities, defined as minorities and women. This was an effort to secure diversity in ownership. However, due to a court ruling, interpreted as requiring the Federal Government to offer only race and gender neutral bid opportunities, the definition of Designated Entities was restricted to include only the race and gender neutral category of small businesses. The challenge was the federal definition of a small business. In the category of telecommunications, a small business referred to those doing less than fifty million dollars ($50,000,000) in annual revenue.

Now the bidding landscaped changed. Those smaller minority and women owned businesses were up against the rural telephone companies looking to acquire spectrum for a wireless business to coincide with their wire line service and they were no longer going to bid against the giant telephone and long distance companies. My strategy was to pursue markets in which we had TV stations. I limited our bid price to a figure I calculated from my due diligence research. After speaking with executives from some of the larger A and B block bidders, I had some confidence in my "not to exceed" number. These larger companies were the regional telephone and long distance companies, such as ATT, Sprint and those now known today as Cingular and Verizon.

Equipped with the knowledge obtained by our research and

having sold a couple of our TV stations to fund this effort, coupled with my Actionaire spirit, Roberts Wireless made its debut. Within a few rounds of the bidding the price exceeded our established limit of fifteen dollars ($15) per population number with the market. Every one of our target cities was eliminated. What do we do? I refused to over pay. The uncertainties were too great. I turned to the experiences I developed in watching the emergence of the cable TV industry.

In the early 1980s I represented one of the largest cable TV companies in the United States. My task was to lobby mayors and councilmen in various large cities to support selecting my client as their cable provider. Only one could win and it required the vote of the mayor and city council. I learned that although all the major cable companies were in competition for the large metropolitan areas, several small companies were easily acquiring the smaller surrounding cities. Later, the large companies, having built out the larger cities, looked to the little communities around them as targets for acquisitions. This created extremely profitable opportunities for those visionary entrepreneurs owning those surrounding small market cable franchises.

With that lesson in mind I directed our PCS bidding into markets surrounding the St. Louis. That strategy worked and we became one of only a couple of successful minority bidders in the auction nationwide.

I am reminded of a quote from one of my favorite movies where a non-political man ran for political office and won. When the news came to him on the outcome of the race his close associate commented, "the good news is we won, and the bad news is we won." This quote summed-up my mixed emotions.

This is a dilemma that faces every successful Actionaire. It is your self-confidence that carriers you past the dilemma and on to triumph.

Once Roberts Wireless was the winner of PCS licenses I knew in order for me to build a wireless phone company, I would need to draw upon my past experiences to solve some major problems, mainly financing, branding and engineering.

When Steven and I built our first TV station, it was understood that to operate a broadcast station, as an independent, in the highly competitive St. Louis market was, at best, futile. I needed to approach the use of our broadcast spectrum a novel way. It was to become television broadcasting, but not with typical programming.

Following a trip to Jamaica for a telecommunications conference for minorities interested in entering the broadcast business, I embarked on a side jaunt to St. Petersburg, Florida, the home of a relatively unknown, budding company. It was the vision of founder/owners Roy Speer and Bud Paxson to have their company expand across the United States. Their plan was to televise it's programming by way of television broadcast affiliates in primarily large markets and the emerging cable companies.

The name of the company is the Home Shopping Network (HSN). I knew immediately that this was the answer for our new venture. We would become one of the early HSN affiliates. HSN provided us with programming, financing, a guaranteed revenue stream and a brand. This blend set the course for our success. We remained the HSN affiliate from 1989 to 2003 when we changed the brand and became the United Paramount Network (UPN) affiliate for St. Louis. The UPN brand lead to another, nearly automatic, success.

Knowledge, opportunity and vision coupled with our high level of self-esteem and Action were the elements of creating these successful business enterprises.

Our wireless opportunity needed to have a brand. Who would know Roberts Wireless in rural Missouri? Would we be able to convince bankers that our business plan will support a Seventy five million dollar ($75,000,000) loan? Could we be first to market with PCS service by building our system rapidly? Would we have a collection component in place in time? These and many more questions joined me in bed every night for weeks.

Everyday I took Action. Sprint PCS was in the throws of building infrastructure in the largest cities in the United States. They were the only company that purchased licenses with full coverage of the United States and its protectorates.

My research discovered that they spent over ten billion dollars ($10,000,000,000) and had not completed the largest cities. I knew that Sprint had plans to cover the entire country and that to achieve this goal they, like HSN, would need affiliates.

After making an appointment with representatives of Sprint, several of my staff and engineering consultants boarded a plane for Kansas City, the home of Sprint. We came in force and impressed their executives with our knowledge of the business, history of our companies and commitment to get the system infrastructure built.

Unfortunately, at the end of the day they informed us that

they were creating affiliates but it was the policy to work exclusively with established rural telephone companies. As the owner of licenses in half the state of Missouri, I did suggest life would be much easier on both of us if we were not competing against each other. I represented to the Sprint executives in a friendly, persuasive and non-threatening manner that I had set my resolve to build Roberts Wireless. My suggestion was that it made all the sense in the world for us to proceed as a team.

Disappointed by this set-back, my team and I packed our bags. I knew however it was not over for us. I stayed in close contact with the Sprint representatives. Not to my surprise, one-day weeks after our non-jubilant trip to the Sprint offices, I received a call from them offering me an invitation for dinner in St. Louis.

Kay Gabbert, our Vice President and my point person on this endeavor escorted me that night. It is highly recommended that you carry your expert to meetings of this nature. I also think it is a good idea to have a witness or second pair of ears. The dinner was engaging and friendly. However, we discovered, before the night was over, that they were there for one reason.

We discussed many small-unrelated things that night, such as sports, politics, and family. In attendance was the head of the St. Louis market, her number two, the director of affiliate relations and his associate. The offer was made and we became one of the first five affiliates of Sprint PCS.

The partnership was announced in the Wall Street Journal. We had changed their policy from only selecting rural telephone companies as affiliates. **Roberts Wireless had become**

Sprint's first non-wire line telephone company entrepreneurial partner.

Following this announcement we became empowered immediately. Bankers viewed us differently, suppliers called upon us, and we were on our way. However, this was not only a new company; it was an emerging field of business. At this point in history, very few bankers knew the meaning or potential of the PCS industry. I made several trips to visit New York investment bankers. When I gave them my vision and plan, they were very polite but offered no financial support.

I tell the story of asking for eighty million dollars ($80,000,000), and needing to step around his desk and pick him up off the floor because he was laughing so hard. That did not stop me.

As our company sold our TV stations to finance the early costs of engineering and building out of our tower sites, switch facilities and stores, I recognized time was running short and we would need much more money to meet our major financial calls.

While searching for a solution, I discovered that it had become common for the large vendors of equipment to finance the build out of PCS operations. As an Actionaire, it was my calling to make something happen.

We needed the best loan terms available. The only way to make this happen was to pit the two large vendors against each other. The winner will have the opportunity to place its equipment in the very important state of Missouri, the home of Sprint. I dangled that carrot and it worked. Lucent Technologies wanted Missouri for strategic reasons. With their loan and equipment we began our build out.

As a Sprint affiliate we were able to meet all of our objectives. We had a brand name with buying power, back office support, collections, and engineering assistance. This support coupled with the fifty six million dollars ($56,000,000) loaned to us by our vendor Lucent closed the loop.

Roberts Wireless was successfully built. Nearing the end of our venture I recognized that this was a company that needed a greater status, one that will carry it into the future. I took another lesson from my past and decided to merge Roberts Wireless with three other Sprint affiliates and go public. Our public offering was a great success. All debt was removed from the Roberts Companies; and stock options were issued to all our employees. My brother and I became members of the Alamosa PCS board of directors and reportedly received over Three hundred and fifty million dollars ($350,000,000) in stock. Additionally, we kept all the telecommunication towers built by us with lease back agreements from the public company; a lesson learned when we sold our TV stations while keeping the broadcast towers.

This PCS transaction resulted in us becoming the largest and most successful Sprint PCS affiliate. Our story garnered international media attention as it was reported in *Forbes, Success, and Black Enterprise* Magazines.

Chapter 6

YOUR FOCAL POINT

What is the center of your being? What internally guides you and gives you outward direction? What is the voice that whispers in your inner ear creating concerns, warning you of possible failure, or signals you to go forward into triumph? Your focal point is your intrinsic center of focus communicated to you through your instincts.

All humans have a focal point; however, we frequently fail to recognize it, or its profound effects on our existence. Your focal point is fastened to your self-image, vision, and work ethic. In order to pursue your calling in life, you must be disciplined in your focal point. Nothing will be accomplished without initially being centered or focused. Failure to utilize or avail yourself of your focal point will render you unstable. As a result, your plans are indistinct and nothing responds to your wants and desires.

Many of your comrades, business associates, and acquaintances, who do not know or have not developed their focal points, habitually suppress their ideas; therefore, they become pawns used for the personal gain of others.

The Actionaire is in tune with their focal point. Actionaires se their focal point's powers to create balance and harmony in every functioning aspect of their personal and business life. In the business world, the Actionaire's focal point is to generate wealth and authority. In our social order, the basic "lynch pin" to achieve success is based on economic security. In life's gamut of essentials, physical survival and financial security are at the top of the list. Needs of lower priority are not considered until these basic wants are minimally satisfied.

Most people are usually doubtful and dubious about the stability and security of their finances. When they solely focus on making money for the sake of surviving, their focal point becomes distracted, and exploitation arises. In order to reach greater possibilities in their life, they must look beyond their minimal needs and expand their focal point.

Once the Actionaire establishes a sturdy economic foundation, they resolve the survival needs of their family and employees. From this foundation, other focal points may be asserted. If this foundation is placed in an unsecured status, the Actionaire will experience some anxiety, uneasiness, and become defensive toward the cause of this threat. The Actionaire will then rely on their positive self-image, clear vision, and relentless work ethic to regain their focal point of generating financial wealth. In order to be disciplined in any focal point, the Actionaire needs an encouraging support system. If the Actionaire has a family, then certain distractions could arise that might deter them from their focal point.

In order to alleviate these distractions and establish their focal point, the Actionaire must convince their family that economic matters come second to familial responsibilities. Actionaires may be perceived as self-centered workaholics; if their loved ones did not support their efforts to the financial betterment of the family, they would consider themselves ineffective in all areas of life. This career-driven focal point must be accomplished while remaining devoted to sustaining the core of the family structure.

If the focal point of an Actionaire is to gain wealth and authority, then how will it be used once acquired? What are the intentions behind this type of focal point?

Often, the driving force of individuals is to possess real estate, cars, jewelry, expensive shoes, designer outfits, planes, and boats. Many people also desire their money to make them socially prominent or famous. There is no real focal point because they are never constant or anchored in reality. Their entire focus centers on protecting their reputation, economic assets, and material possessions, which are illusions. Losing their fortunes and fame could lead them to a life of insanity or worse.

The Actionaire knows that if their focal point results in these types of material or social objectives, a defect exists. They recognize and understand that all these bits and pieces of wealth can vanish rapidly. If their life is defined by reputation or items of ownership, then it will remain in a constant state of peril and jeopardy because these possessions may be lost, stolen, or devalued. When these superficial people are in the presence of a more affluent person who has a higher fame, net worth, or greater status, they feel inferior. The reverse is true if they are in the company of an impoverished person. The Actionaire's self-worth is constant; it does not fluctuate because they are defined in terms of family and familial responsibilities and not in terms of their own reputation, ownership, or social standing.

The Actionaire's position is a simple one. While having material possessions and fame is fun and enjoyable, it is not life's panacea. Instant gratification is obtainable and encouraged in our society. With mass media constantly displaying marketable illusions, the allure of fame and wealth increase expectations. Living the life style of the rich and famous seems within an easy grasp, but seldom, the real story is accurately seen. Through productivity, building relationships, and strengthening the inner person, the Actionaire defects this glitter of bliss and constructs a meaningful life.

Guiltless diversions in moderation can provide relaxation for the body and mind, and can foster family and other relationships. These loving and affectionate moments of family exchanges are appreciated, however, the Actionaire's enjoyments offer no profound, lasting happiness or sense of accomplishment. The Actionaire avoids the narcissistic way of life. When fun is your only focus, then that one level of pleasure ultimately creates boredom and will eventually drive you to a new higher level of pleasure. This drive continues until life is interpreted by the pleasures you find.

Staying in the casino for hours or days, watching too many videos, movies, or television, or visiting the beach day after day is the behavior of non-productive people. This spending of undisciplined leisure time or taking the path of least resistance results in an insignificant life. If this behavior continues, it ensures that your calling or potential remains dormant, your talents remain untapped, and your focal point stays blurred or non-existent. In turn, the mind and soul become lethargic, and life's passions are unsatisfied.

"Nothing in the world can take the place of persistence. Talent will not. Nothing is more common than unsuccessful men with talent. Genius will not. Un-rewarded genius is almost a proverb. Education will not. The world is full of educated derelicts. Persistence, determination, and hard work make the difference."- Calvin Coolidge.

Church-Spirituality

The Actionaire has a spiritual focal point. Frequently, individuals who obsessively engage in church worship and projects become insensitive to the immediate human problems that surround them. Often, those holier than thou religious zealots' behavior contradicts the very precepts they profess to believe. Some people, who attend religious services less often or not at all, will exhibit behavior that reflects a more clear focus on the teachings of their faith's doctrines.
Personal spirituality is not synonymous with church attendance.

Actionaires are consistent and faithful to the teaching of their religion. The Actionaire is unlike other individuals who strive for image and appearance by being active in the church meetings, but hypocritically revert to opposite behavior in their daily life. The Actionaire knows that such beliefs and behaviors are insincere, destructive, and undermine their focal point.

Frequently in the world of business and politics, you find these people who make church their dominant consideration. They make the church organization the focus of their life, image, and appearance. They tend to artificially label you with "trumped up" and exaggerated terms: liberal, conservative, moderate, orthodox, unorthodox, feminist, chauvinist, unholy, abortionist, right wing, left wing, or centrist. They fail to realize that the church is a formal organization made up of policies, programs, practices, traditions, and people. They make the error of considering the church as a place that creates some inborn value.

The Actionaire's focal point is to live the principles learned through their spiritual training. They know that belonging to an organization will not provide them with their focal point or center. They understand that living without a focal point and depending on the church or any organization to create their intrinsic value causes them to live in compartments. This inconsistency in these religious zealots' function and behavior produces social imbalance, reduced personal integrity, and the inability to find their focal point. Without a focal point, one finds the need to self-justify their Actions, which results in the labeling of others.

The church or any organization is not an end in itself, rather a means to an end. The Actionaire views their spirituality as an essential component of their purpose. Even though the church claims to teach people about the origin of power, it does not claim to be that power in and of itself. The Actionaire understands that the church is a vehicle through which divine power can be awakened in humans.

Chapter 7

GENETIC CODE:
THE FLESH VS. THE MIND

Does a preordained force of nature govern you? Does your heredity presuppose how you are to exist? Was your destiny fashioned in advance?

The Actionaire has a vision to pursue, a calling to accomplish, and a destiny to encounter. Is the completion of these objectives foreknown? Is your life predestined or do you simply create your life's experiences in the moment of now? Divine nature follows a remarkable genetic pattern of equally distributing intelligence among its human creation. If an Intelligence Quota Test were given today, various amounts of people would be tested with high, medium, and low intelligence. Everyone has intelligence, but some people choose to tap into it more than others. It has been reported that dissimilar individuals learn best in different ways: orally, visually, or through written communications. Every person has a significant contribution to bestow upon our social order. However, society fails to equally distribute access to education, training, and opportunity to its citizens. Can you succeed in gaining authority and wealth by simply allowing nature to take its course? Will your genetic code guarantee or protect your ability to achieve?

Medical science has reported that each of us has a genetic code. As we learn more about our genetics, the more information we infer about our individual physical and mental conditions. If our ancestors or immediate relatives were diabetic, had heart aliments, breast cancer, or sickle cell anemia, we can possibly prevent symptoms in advance by eating well, exercising, and having routine physical exams. Nevertheless, only taking Action upon this information can provide you with any offered protections.

The Actionaire aggressively protects their body. Having your health monitored is crucial to your long-term survival. Genetic codes may influence behavior and attitudes. If we evaluate our behavior, attitudes, and reactions toward events and occurrences, we will observe certain basic and repetitive traits. For example, you might have vowed during your adolescence to never be like your parents; however, you inevitably repeat their Actions and behaviors throughout your adulthood.

Academic, social, and economic environments mold your methods of delivering the same, basic traits. Nevertheless, when the Actionaire desires to take steps to change their life's direction or seek their purpose, they realize that Action is mandatory. A change in their attachment to the status quo or "norm" immediately places them squarely on the horns of a dilemma. Conflicting issues cause this predicament. The issues are presented by the desires of the flesh and the rational of the mind.

An example of a dilemma would be making the choice between eating a piece of your favorite chocolate while on your diet or eating a non-fat soy bar. The quandary arises from two conflicting issues. The chocolate tastes good but causes your body fat content to rise; the non-tasty soy bar is healthy and non-fattening.

Your code tells you to eat the chocolate, but your mind says eat the soy bar. The Actionaire would not find themselves in a perplex battle that may lead to them either following the flesh, the mind, or doing nothing. The Actionaire would choose, but with a compromise. If the chocolate is eaten, a physical work out must be planned and executed to balance the desires of the flesh and the rational of the mind. If the soy bar is eaten, then another desire of the flesh is indulged to meet that need. On an extreme scale, following the mind or the flesh may cause the Actionaire problems in fulfilling their drive to gain authority and wealth. The Actionaire must remain balanced between the two conflicts.

As we learn more about our genetics, we discover that the elements in the flesh are connected to the past generations. For example, if your relatives suffer from alcoholism and drug addiction, then you are predisposed to potentially mirror the same or other types of addictive behavior. When your conduct benefits the flesh, it originates from your genetic coding. The flesh directs your mind, and the mind directs your behavior. If you are under the directions of the code, then you will experience the confinement of the "normalcy," which gives you the balance to merely survive in our present civilization. The "normalcy" of our society is rooted in consumerism. Consumerism is the craving of the flesh. With independence of mind, you will not be conditioned by society's basic program of existence.

The Actionaire reaches authority and wealth through independent Action and experimentation. The Actionaire's mind leads their flesh to connect with Action. You are naturally coded to lean away from Action, hold on to the status quo, and remain stagnated. The Actionaire conquers this weakness that directs the flesh to do only the simple things in life.

There is a battle going on inside of us. We are torn between following the direction of the flesh and the calling in the mind and spirit. The conflict is between your mental restraints and your human desires. Mental restraint is spiritually guided. Human desires are carnally directed.

The Actionaire constantly faces the difficult challenge of attaining authority and wealth. They are constantly fighting for their vision, calling, and destiny, which are formed by the mind and genetic coding. Humans are also genetically set up to pursue the carnal needs and are satisfied by appealing and appeasing the flesh. This dilemma is our genetic disposition. The flesh coaches you on mere survival tactics and the mind guides you to a consequential life.

Our civilization is an organized mechanism used to place the populace into a sociologically and economically controlled surrounding. This milieu patterns your behavior and Actions to its prototype. This imprisonment keeps your carnal drives accepting only the basics, while living a socially acceptable and substantially restricted life style. The caveat is that these signals and instructions may create a clash between your calling and your code.

The Actionaire, responding to his society and his raw desires, compromises by being balanced between the genetic coding of his flesh and the mystical calling of the mind. The Actionaire makes a healthy choice to apply his mind's restraint, while moderately indulging his flesh. The Actionaire is internally guided and externally directed into victory.

Chapter 8

AVOID THE UTILITARIAN LIFE

ONE LIFE: PERSONAL AND BUSINESS

The Actionaire's personal and business lives are one. They mentally link them differently, but with limited distinction. Often, the Actionaire's relatives, friends, and coworkers do not understand the Actionaire's life plan. They do not see the truth in its entirety.

The Actionaire believes that building one's business or career is just as important and rewarding as family vacations and children's graduations. The Actionaire's behavior appears to be insensitive because they frequently contradict the lessons taught by the family, religious, and educational structures; they challenge the societal rules of separating work and play.

Generally, we are taught to become an uninteresting, lackluster, repetitive, or monotonous utilitarian. You are instructed to live a life that is practical, useful, and robotically serviceable to society. You must obediently perform your no-frills 9-to-5 jobs, enjoy your two week vacation, and plan a retirement.

To become an Actionaire, you will be obliged to shatter this rule. You must be prepared to ward off the onslaught of society's status quo disciples. Confronting them requires a mind set that is resolute to your vision. You must be capable of challenging this constrained societal and workplace environment. These limited environs require you to quit your passion for business and approach life in a traditional and predictable way. These restrictive settings are positioned to detach your mind from that multi-tiered, diverse existence adored by you and force you into a conventional subsistence. This conformed surrounding hinders the Actionaire's growth and will ultimately robotize them.

Most friends and family members don't have the vision or drive to fulfill their calling. They do not understand an Actionaire's behavior, which makes it virtually impossible for the Actionaire to communicate the reason of their Actions. The realism of an Actionaire's psyche is that they consider the love and comfort of family and friends as the foundation for their survival and existence. Without their family's support, their home life and business ambitions would lack purpose.

It's unfortunate that so many people see life as an occurrence guided by a mystical existence and not by the choices they make. Scapegoat phrases like " I guess it was meant to be" are avoided by the Actionaire and embraced by individuals who use crutches on which to lean when poor decisions are made or even when they hit the winning lottery number.

Most people don't understand the era in which they live. They see their life as either being guided by a higher being or as a series of accidents linked together.

The Actionaire sees life as a link of choices. They envision life as a series of confrontations with precise Action being the weapon of choice to succeed. The Actionaire understands only one-word,

ACTION, and respects only two words, Wealth and Authorit

Action achieves personal wealth and authority. It is ...c wealthy and those with authority that carry the clout, which controls and directs people with power.

POWER IS FLEETING; AUTHORITY ENDURES

Power is the ability to achieve work through others, whether they are willing or not.

Authority is the ability of a person or organization to achieve work through people that believe in the legitimacy of his or its position and their acceptance of it.

A person or organization might have Power but not the legitimacy required to effectively exercise Authority. Only Action leads to Authority. When Dr. Martin Luther King, Jr. began his quest for civil rights, the "state" held all of the Power. Dr. King's Actions ultimately achieved legitimacy within American society that overwhelmed the Power of the state. Thus, Power not only succumbed to Authority, the Authority of Dr. King's Actions became the Power.

The complexity and importance of gaining wealth and authority will be understood once you become an Actionaire. Whatever has not been done in your life is only that which you have not taken Action upon. Achieving your goals and dreams is possible if you keep in mind that ACTION HAS NO SEASON.

Chapter 9

THE PARADOX

The dynamics of gaining authority and wealth may require Actions that were deemed as boorish and distasteful throughout your childhood. As children, we were taught "manners," which were to respect everyone, "turn the other cheek" in any altercation, and never lie. The concepts in this chapter defy most of these childhood rules and nullify the image of "ideal behavior."

Nobody is ever as they first appear. Packaging is deceptive. Book covers can make a drab book look like the most exciting book on the planet. Billions of dollars are expended on appearances. Looks are very important because appearance alone has the power to sell or discourage. Creating a climate of acceptance is important in any business transaction. The person behind the deal is more important than the packaging of their appearance. In business, you must emit an air of approval toward the other person in the transaction. Nothing is ever as it first appears. Start observing the body language and attitude of the people in the deal. Listen for their needs. Don't misjudge them.

Your first impression is always limited. It is possibly very wrong. Stop prejudging people. Only fools make permanent decisions without knowledge. Never assume your intuition or perception is always correct. Actionaires never judge people by their outward appearance. Your success in business should never be impeded by prejudice, fear, or any form of discrimination. The Actionaire never discriminates against a person because of their race, gender, financial status, or appearance. Never eliminate anyone from the chain of your success.

People seeking more authority must understand the dangers within the paradox of gaining authority. It is a constant dynamic of being cunning while polite, devious yet fair, and magnanimous but selfish. History teaches us that people of great authority surrounded themselves with other people who believe in this unspoken, contradictious rule.

During the days of the Great Roman Empire, messengers were killed for delivering bad news, even if the news was vital to the survival and future of the empire.

In the business environment, leaders always play the sport of constant duplicity. In the scheming world of corporate life, this control mechanism is inherent amongst those in leadership positions. The lower level devotee is particularly placed in a delicate position. If the devotee excels in their duties for the leader and their Actions curry favor in obvious ways, their cohorts will notice and plot against them.

Yet, the company environment is supposed to represent the height of cooperation and team spirit. In reality, lesser Action-oriented persons will nevertheless work silently and secretly against any associate who attempts to advance above their level. These individuals frown frequently upon overt, forceful moves.

Herein lays the paradox of the corporate culture faced by

employees, entrepreneurs, political aspirants, and capitalists. On the surface of the corporate world, everyone must peacefully coexist with each other; therefore, everything must appear conventional, politically correct, and civilized. If you strictly play by the rules, then you can be assured that the clever ones will stampede you. Taking a direction that is clear and identifiable to your rivals gives those individuals a target to attach, a plan to steal, or an opportunity to rob. The best approach is to assume a casual image, which suggests that you are blasé, nonchalant, detached, laid-back, indifferent, and uncertain. There is nothing wrong with setting a goal and strategically planning for it. The Actionaire should remain sure of their plan, but does not emerge overly confident or convinced. On occasion, the Actionaire should display mistakes or admit to faults. Envy by individuals will create asserted, negative Action. It is smart to masquerade your strengths by demonstrating a weakness to your antagonist.

My interest is to shape you into a shrewd corporate executive, an astute entrepreneur, a hard-core capitalist, or a clever political insurgent. In the past, you may have heard "honesty is the best policy and that virtue is its own reward".

If you subscribe to this doctrine and have been forever wedged in your job, stagnant in your business, or experiencing a boring lifestyle, then it's time for you to take Action and face the reality that some people are consciously and consistently playing control games with you. In order to be inconspicuous, these masked moves are often placed on you in an indirect manner. Some of the most adept manipulators express their opinions outwardly. By behaving oppositely from their objective to dominate you, they convince you that they no longer want a position of authority.

One strategy is to treat everyone equally and demand equality for all. This pretender cloaks his or her move to gain authority by appearing to treat everyone equally and fairly. They minister to everyone evenly and pay no heed to their differences. This deceit bumps up the less skillful and curbs those with unique talent. It also creates an inferior self-esteem in the honest person.

The Actionaire is always faintly commanding attention thereby reinforcing the presence of leadership. Through their calm and collective nature, the Actionaire's persona appears larger than that of their devotee. The Actionaire must at all times remain above reproach.

If our society was perfect or practiced perfection and did not take part in the domination game, one could engage in straightforwardness and fair cooperation. However, the main techniques of authority seekers are concealment and trickery. History, unfortunately, has taught that straightforwardness and truth may inadvertently hurt or destroy us. The irony in the life of some individuals is that they may ultimately serve the very Actionaire who suppressed their opportunity to succeed. Most people avoid truth. The Actionaire recognizes truth and reality, but continues to play the game of duplicity. In order to succeed in our society, the Actionaire stays balanced in every aspect of life; therefore, they are not an extreme of anything. Life is tough and difficult. Addressing the dreams of people endears you to them. The Actionaire will foster the support of those individuals by removing them from their boring, disenchanted, or stagnate lives.

Great controls are gained through involvement in the imaginations of people.

If you are trapped in this society of duplicity, do you try to opt out or do you become an Actionaire? Ignoring or struggling against the inevitable will only lead to continued failures, mediocrity, depression, guilt, unhappiness, and possibly poverty. Instead, you must take Action to access authority and wealth. By becoming an Actionaire, you will release the potential within you.

Your attitude will determine your altitude of wealth and authority.

Chapter 10

MASTERING YOUR EMOTIONS

Controlling your emotions is the first step to becoming an Actionaire. The single greatest detriment to acquiring authority and influence comes through the failure of mastering your emotions. An inappropriate response to a disagreeable situation or business deal could change your life instantly. The momentary gratification of exposing your attitude is not worth your life's work. Acting impulsively by divulging your emotions could cost your perseverance and dedication to acquiring authority and wealth. If you keep your focus on the "big picture," which is your calling, vision, and destiny, then you will never be hurt or experience any extreme emotion.

A person who demonstrates anger portrays the most destructive response to a state of affairs. Rage and unbridled tempers impair your vision more than any emotion. The opposite side of the emotional spectrum is love, worship, and enticement. If used in an extreme manner, both emotions could be equally destructive. These emotions cloud the path to your objective and could position you in an ill-fated predicament. It is improbable and nearly impossible to modify love or anger, and you would probably be unsuccessful if you tried. You should never allow these emotions to influence your Actions or strategies to gain financial freedom and influence.

Mastering your emotions requires you to detach yourself from the moment and become mindful of the future ramifications of your Actions. Avoiding surprises can guarantee control of your emotional reaction to any state of affairs. In order to avoid surprises, you must plan a reaction to any possible situation. Live and breathe the phrase, "never let them see you sweat".

The Actionaire does not hold grudges nor retain past disappointments. In fact, they must release old disappointments. Past thoughts may keep you locked to the experience of the past. Thoughts of the past may distract you and affect your reasoning. Studying the past, however, will allow you to examine mistakes that have caused previous problems. Self -evaluation will enable you to break past behavior and lead you to a new course of Action. Releasing the past will lead you to the gifts of the present and future. Actionaires understand themselves and know how to control their representations of self. Through high self-esteem, they accept and approve of themselves.

Conducting a performance of different appearances is a skill you must develop to acquire authority and wealth. The art of duplicity requires you to wear many faces. As a human, you are superior to every other living creature. A person has a natural ability to mislead, stretch the truth, and trick their fellow humans. Deception is an extremely potent weapon and your emotional control is your barrier of protection.

Opportunity will always find your doorstep if you look only slightly into the future. It is the patience that you apply to your situation that makes you strong, and it is impatience that makes you weak.

When opportunities are presented, an Actionaire's approach may be considered unprincipled or unscrupulous. They must evaluate this situation not as good or evil. An Actionaire does not judge their opponents by their words or Actions; rather, the judgment is based only on the net effect of their Action.

The paragon of decency is your appearance, while actually being the manipulator of all time is your true persona. Understanding your opponent's hidden motives is the most profound bit of data you can acquire and is the key for all negotiations.

Always take the indirect road to achieving authority. A cunning camouflage of your Action begins with a detailed analysis of the psychological weakness of your challenger. The art of masquerading is one of the fundamental tools used by the Actionaire.

Chapter 11

SUMMON YOUR MOTIVATION

Motivation

Actionaires are self-motivated. Some people have a tough time motivating themselves. One would think that the incentive of success, achievement, and fulfillment of your greatest dreams would propel you into Action. However, self-induced Action is a major problem for some individuals. Self-motivation is key to achieving your goals in life.

Enthusiasm is needed when we desire a result, but we do not feel inspired to act upon it. The secret to summoning motivation lies within you. It is your drive to pursue your goal because you yearn for completion and success. What is the most effective strategy that an Actionaire deploys to awaken their motivation?

The Actionaire envisions the desirable outcome of their achievement. The ever-present distractions of parties, theme parks, fun trips, and great theater will not stifle their relentless vigor to succeed. They clearly visualize their path to success and choose to stay focused even amongst the allure of momentary fun. In the end, momentary fun pales in comparison to the richness of completing their business dreams. The Actionaire pictures their objectives in clear, compelling detail and imagines the wonderful feeling of accomplishment.

Actionaires' inspiration is a precursor to success; it is a self rewarding effort. Our society embraces motivated people who set goals and work toward their objectives. Positive stimulation moves a businessperson towards wealth and authority. The religious, educational, and familial institutions impress morals and values into your mind. You must be conscious of your own values in order to find your motivation. It is difficult to find motivation when you are conducting business activities that you find immoral or boring. Your morals and values are the important motivating factors that keep you in focus.

If the venture is unattractive or uncomfortable, you will not find the necessary motivation to maximize the endeavor. You must determine what is important versus what is not important. It is natural for you to increase that which you prefer and decrease that which you abhor. You will increase your likes and decrease your dislikes. Knowing your preferences and aggressively pursuing those aspirations naturally provide you with the necessary drive to proceed. The reverse is true for the person working in an undesirable environment.

Carrying out impassioned endeavors makes your business efforts more focused and successful. Your choice of business ventures must be compelling and attractive to you. You will become a motivated Actionaire when your values and principles work in concert with your business efforts.

Real success is not a destination, but a journey. The Actionaire's motivation to succeed is not only measured in terms of possessions, popularity, and performance, but in acting or doing out of sheer enjoyment. The pure love of Action and movement impels the Actionaire. Experiencing progress creates enjoyment. Daily motivation to succeed encompasses the joys of today, the gift of the present, and the moment of now. The Actionaire understands their life's assignment.

Success has ambiguous interpretations. People define it differently at distinct times in their lives. As an example, you offer your three year old daughter a lady's Rolex watch on her birthday, and she displays a level of disappointment. If she was offered a soft stuffed teddy bear, you might discover that this stuffed animal was the best gift for her.

On the other hand, once the same little girl grows and matures, her desires and goals will change. It is nineteen years later, and she is graduating from college. If you were to now offer here the same teddy bear, she would be very disappointed. It would not be her idea of a great graduation gift. She now becomes interested in the offer of a Rolex watch.

The Actionaire realizes that true success is achieving the goals presently before them. Many people lose motivation in life; therefore, they stop growing along the way. Instead of realizing their potential to prosper and be successful, they sit back with their teddy bear and wonder why they find very little satisfaction in life.

It is possible to impulsively act ahead of your growth schedule. They try to grab the Rolex watch before they know how to tell time. Due to their misdirected priority focus at their level of growth, they become dissatisfied with their achievements. Life has a rhythm and your growth process is aligned with its beat.

Patience is the key to becoming one with the rhythm of life. All events and Actions have their time of occurrence. Being patient and acting accordingly to your time will lead to your success. Success, like most things, is relative. Success means diverse results to different people at various moments. The Actionaire seeks to recognize their point of growth on their life's journey.

The Actionaire learns to enjoy their momentary possessions instead of dwelling on their "wish list" of unobtainable items. Their motivation is focused on achieving growth and personal satisfaction with their life.

The Actionaire's mind is composed of certain stimulating factors. This type of mind creates success. The factors that produce success consist of persistence, discipline, and integrity. You need to uphold a code of honesty to self. Remain true to the indispensable factors within you.

Through the discipline of work, Actionaires accumulate wealth and authority. No one tells the Actionaire when to wake up and initiate the day. They arise everyday obsessed with self-motivation and an internal commitment to their mission to cultivate wealth and authority.

Chapter 12

YOUR INNER CONSTITUTION

The Actionaire's personal philosophy metaphysically argues that the definition of a true capitalist's essence must follow the estimation and recognition of their existence. Some individuals are oblivious to the present. They generally function with thoughts of the nonexistent, which are rooted in a state of nothingness. Whether it's in the past, the future, or a different world, they live their lives in fantasies. They exist often in an unclear fog. This self-deception inhibits them from taking Action. They become comfortable in their own fantasies. These people are mainly followers. They never look past the surface or dig deep within themselves to understand their true existence. Sometimes, these complacent individuals cry for deliverance from the fears of the here and now. They fight against facing anything but the facts immediately before them.

The environment of the Actionaire is not one of mild tones and soft lights. The sounds are loud and piercing, and the light is bright and glaring. In the societies' "normal" environment, any self-deception, regardless of degree, can justify a departure from negative or unpleasant facts. An Actionaire understands and faces their inner self, which consists of moods, anxieties, and fears. In the face of materialist infatuations and tempting circumstances, they find their center and remain uncompromised until these distractions move away.

The Actionaire is an individual. They are aggressive thinkers who are intrigued and fascinated by the virtue of their individuality. In order to live up to their individuality, the Actionaire must be decisive at all times. Being decisive is usually determined by one's reasoning skills or ethics. However, Actionaires will make a decision regardless of the crucial differences between informed and uninformed, reasoned and un-reasoned, and responsible and irresponsible. The Actionaire knows that reasoning alone cannot aid them in the process of decision-making.

Some individuals try to escape the need for choices by conveniently focusing on surface rationalizations. They turn away from making decisions based on excuses like proud traditions or ethics. They have deceived themselves into thinking that they have shouldered the weight of a crucial decision, but they still make a decision by not making a decision. These decisions are also frequently made as a result of veiled or invalid manifestations of the truth. They make
decisions based on their physical reality. They believe that reasoning is the safe, reliable, and conservative way of existing. Merely existing is their plight in life.

The Actionaire does not rashly renounce clear and distinct thinking altogether. They avoid the trivialities that may consume their thoughts. Instead, they concentrate on blending reason and passion, logic and ethics, and mathematics and myth. The

Actionaire realizes that all understanding is not attainable. They must be satisfied with beliefs that cannot be questioned or proven. Taking the leap of faith in business does not mean that one will not consider the truth and facts. They do not see faith as the archenemy of reason. An Actionaire is simply an apostle of passion and a critic of hypocrisy. They do not extol passion at the expense of reason. The Actionaire remains balanced in every aspect of their life. They consider all possibilities.

There is an inner constitution that the Actionaire possesses. Their truth is a paradox of subjectivity and objectivity. If their decision requires long meditation or requires development, it is abandoned. Frequently, their decisions are offered abruptly and dogmatically, but are labeled as subjective because of the conviction and confidence in its delivery. Although they may listen to other points of view, they consider other people's feelings to be on a different level than their own. To guard against the perspective of another, they do not risk their position. The Actionaire elevates above reason by envisioning their mission through personal rationale. It is this leap of faith that makes the Actionaire rise above the skeptics and soar higher than the fog that engulfs them. It is this metaphysical understanding upon which a visionary depends. This comprehension is the knowledge that they intercept through interpretation of their internal self and external surroundings.

The Actionaire is inclined to govern and lead through faith and decisive behavior. Actionaires not only manage change, but they are comfortable with it in their own lives. They understand the simple principle that they can chance

or take risks that will provide improvement, enhancement, cultivation, and refinement of their undeveloped skills and talents.

Chapter 13

NATURAL RHYTHMS;
UNDERSTANDING YOUR TIME

The Actionaire recognizes their time to take Action. This realization propels them into producing effective, efficient, and valuable decisions during these periods. They manage these transitional stages with precision.

Understanding is the grasping of knowledge. Astuteness is the application of that knowledge. Most individuals' greatest weakness is ignorance or lack of information. The unmotivated and unsuccessful individuals believe that their lives will never change; therefore, they fail to anticipate or adjust to future environmental transformations. This rejection of change will disable their authority and wealth in society and life.

Actionaires know that they must change with the evolution of their environment. The natural rhythms that permeate their environment alert them to the possibility of change. In response to feeling a shift in these natural rhythms, the Actionaire takes Action. All life forms are connected and have a natural insight into each other, which is expressed through our power of intuition. We choose to actively respond to our intuition. This form of intuitive acceptance releases the power of our instincts.

In the business and social world of the Actionaire, certain inherent rules apply. Transformation is inevitable and guaranteed. It consistently occurs throughout the transition of time. When two or more people converge, one can presuppose that differing options and opinions will surface. These differences indicate the non-permanent nature of a social or business relationship. The two people in the business setting will have to reach a compromise in order to agree. Within some time period, change will occur. When interacting with another person, you will have to adjust your Actions to agree with their boundaries. All existence functions within temporary conditions. Nothing and no one can remain the same; only transformation is eternal. Action suggests that present conditions are subject to time and exist within the parameters of a predetermined time period. Time will bring about change, and your choice to act upon that change will determine the progress and time length of your present conditions.

Transitions are always occurring in both the business and social world of the Actionaire. The Actionaire recognizes opportunity when changes are taking place. Not all change creates opportunity, but without change, there can be no opportunity.

Liberation

To access opportunity, you must liberate your mind. Liberation is the absence of restriction. No one gives liberation to you. Many unmotivated people believe that another person possesses their liberation and can bestow emancipation upon them; however, true liberation can never be given to you. You solely achieve your liberation.

What is true liberation? In order to characterize liberation, one must first identify its foundation. When an individual approaches someone to get their liberation, they have just given that person control over their existence. This type of self-imprisonment may be the greatest misconception and weakness of some as they struggle through life. They preserve a form of psychological slavery; oppressed and under the control of the Actionaire. These passive individuals are controlled through psychological intimidation and propaganda.

When submissive individuals allow this dominance to persist, the oppressor will grant them a tainted view of liberation. Some individuals greatly increase their vulnerability to psychological bondage and exploitation throughout their life.

If you presume someone has the authority to extend you liberation, you have just given that person the liberty to control you. They are given the authority to extend to you the autonomy to succeed.

The Actionaire would never give the privilege of ascribing or assigning their value to another person. If you get your self-value from someone else, then they can determine how much you are worth.

Liberation is freedom. Freedom is not something you receive from someone. It is an internal empowerment solely achieved by your choices in life. An Actionaire can never be bound. Liberation is a personal discovery of the truth about you; therefore, liberation is not granted to you, rather it is created by you. Liberating your mind, understanding your time and taking Action will deliver a level of success in your endeavors never imagined.

You are the architect of your life.

A PERSONAL ANECDOTE

Managing the transition........

In the fall of 1979, Ebony Magazine wrote a feature story entitled "The Dynamic Duo, Roberts Brothers Pack One-Two Punch as St. Louis Lawmakers." The basis of the article stemmed from the fact that we were the only brother team on a major city council in the United States.

Embedded in this story was a brief history of our family and business. It spoke of the closeness of our parents, wives, children and extended family members. Regarding our businesses, it wrote of the vision we had for this emerging company and offered quotes from our small business clients and political constituents.

Ebony Magazine is a well-respected and recognized periodical with an international distribution. Resulting from a review of this article a reader contacted me. The caller was a representative of the Sears Corporation. During the late 1970's and through the mid 1980's, Sears made a concerted effort to close all of its inner city stores. This caused a major negative economic impact on the African American communities in the largest cities in America. Chicago, Detroit, Newark, and Los Angeles, where examples and these communities suffered as a result of the Sears exodus. St. Louis was no exception.

Sears made efforts to soften its impact on St. Louis by contacting the local Urban League. They wanted the Urban League to purchase the building and turn it into a community service center. The problem as that the Urban League didn't have the money nor the "know how" to make it work. They are a community service organization and not a real estate developer.

The call I received from Sears was a surprise. They wanted a different acquirer of the property. When asked if we might have an interest in purchasing this huge building, only three blocks from my birthplace, I gave the appropriate Actionaire response, YES. However, there was one hurdle to jump. I wanted to know, directly from the Urban League, whether they had rebuffed the deal.

Why the hesitation? Why not have immediate strikes on this deal? Because keeping our emerging good reputation with the community came first with us. We chose not to be pitted against the Urban League for the purchase of this property. I, instead, paid a visit to my friends, the local president, and the chairman of the St. Louis chapter of the Urban League.

This meeting's agenda consisted of me informing them of the telephone call I received from Sears. They were astonished by this news. Sears had not given them any clue as to their disposition or desires to cancel their arrangement. I made it absolutely clear that we would not interfere with their deal. However, faced with the prospect of losing this deal I extracted a pledge from them. The Urban League agreed, in principal, that if they opted out of this transaction, they would inform us, and we would renew our interest to proceed with the due diligence necessary for the acquisition.

Nearly ten months later I received another call regarding this property. This time it was a conference call with both Sears and the president of the Urban League.

The property known then as the Old Sears Building in north St. Louis consisted of a 200,000 square foot, four level building, with an adjacent auto repair facility, and nearly six acres of parking. The same questions arose when this deal became available. We have heard them over and over again. How do we finance this deal? What will we do with this building? What is the management stratagem? Is this deal accretive to our portfolio?

I knew one important thing, the location of this property was chosen by Sears. This was not only their largest store in the city; it housed their regional offices. Equipped with very little knowledge or experience of commercial and retail real estate, I heavily relied upon the three rules of real estate: "Location, location, location".

Roberts Brothers Properties was formed in 1982 to purchase this old Sears department store building. The old Sears building threatened to become a symbol of the pervasive economic depression that plagued St. Louis' inner city. By 1985, under our business leadership and hard work, this building had become a thriving commercial center, delivering goods and services to more than 3,000 people per day.

This edifice had 50,000 square feet of space per floor. Our vision was to create, what I called, an "urban mall." This urban mall was designed with large hallways creating spaces on each side allowing stores, shops and offices to populate the floors. Tenants of varying types, ranging from the Missouri Department of Revenue, a dentist, counseling assistance for welfare mothers, tax services, a TV station, cosmetics, clothing stores and an auto sound system company are a few of the tenant types. We even boast of our Barbeque/Soul Food and Chinese restaurants.

Over time we have leased space to over 200 tenants. This is why I call it the most diversified urban mall in the country. Under our ownership it became St. Louis' largest commercial office building outside of the downtown business district.

This facility was known as the old Sears Building for several years until we changed the name to the person who worked the hardest in managing our growth and appeasing the tenants, our father, Victor Roberts. So today this building is known as the Victor Roberts Building. My position is simple, Dad deserved it. After all, why should I allow for Mr. Sears to carry his name on my building when all his company did for our community was move out when African Americans moved in?

Successfully revitalizing this commercial center is best exemplified by our ability to create innovative financing strategies and recruit a mix of tenants, which maximized social and economic benefits for the community. In 1991, we added significantly to our community's economic progress with the opening of a new Aldi Supermarket, the largest Aldi store in the state of Missouri, constructed on the corner of the building's parking lot. In 1999, we developed the 14,000 square foot out parcel adjacent to the building, attracting Blockbuster Video into the African American community for the first time. This development also includes a Domino's Pizza and State Farm Insurance office.

Understanding the rhythm of our time was important in inventing and growing our business. It became clear to Steve and me that real estate would serve as an anchor for our future. We felt a change was taking place as a result of our labors. This was a major parcel of property located in our childhood neighborhood and only a mile from our homes. Without taking Action on this property, an already deteriorating community would be facing an even more difficult existence. A 200,000 square foot empty monolith would only have caused that neighborhood to fall further into a vast crevice of decay.

Our advances in the positive growth of the site continued by the acquisition of over ten acres buttressing the Victor Roberts Building and culminated with building The Shops at Roberts Village.

Roberts Village, debuted on January 15, 2003, is an open air 42,000 square foot upscale shopping center. When we christened this area the Roberts Village I based it on the old African proverb "it takes a village to raise a child." My paraphrase is "it takes a village to raise a business." In order, for this community to return to its "hey day," it will need commerce supported by the people in the area. The Roberts Village has created scores of jobs and an improved tax base. Perhaps most importantly people have a place in their neighborhood to shop for goods and services.

Being Opportunistic in the Transforming Environment...

By the 1990's we were on a roll. Our next venture was the acquisition and enhancement of a retail development just one mile away from the Victor Roberts Building. Purchased as an under performing and financially strapped strip shopping center and freestanding grocery store on the edge of St. Louis' fashionable central west-end, it met the rules of real estate acquisition. These properties were owned by an African American not for profit group, known as the Union Sarah Redevelopment Corporation. A one-time strong force in the revitalization of this area during the 1970's, they grew complacent and lacked the aspiration to continue. However, their leader was committed to selling these properties to an eligible African American entity. We were that entity.

Once again equipped with the mindset of an Actionaire, we assessed this prospect. Our evaluation was that this would be accretive to our portfolio. Because it was opportunistic, we acquired this unique property located at one of the busiest intersections in the city. Now on our way to emerging a brand in the real estate business, we labeled this development Roberts Plaza.

This property was uniquely challenged with problems of deferred maintenance, back taxes and non-paying tenants. Moving in quickly, we gave it the face-lift it needed and began negotiations with high end retailers. Though admittedly lacking in experience, our success was instituted through taking Action. We successfully recruited a Hollywood Video store and several specialty retailers such as Street Legends, Rainbow and Payless Shoe Store to fill the strip center.

The rhythm of the time was sending signals.....

As former St. Louis Aldermen, Steven and I learned that a key to the revitalization of a major city requires a robust and vital downtown. Following, our experiences in the central and north sectors of St. Louis, we turned our sites toward downtown. Knowing of the ground swell of interest in downtown living throughout the nations' large cities, I began a search for strategic downtown properties.

The St. Louis Board of Education Office Building was a beautiful seven story vacant structure. Built in 1884, this building was a perfect target for our acquisition. It also met our plans to restore landmark properties. Placed on the historic registry, it was eligible for state and federal historic tax credits. These credits created the opportunity to recover nearly four million dollars ($4,000,000) of our cost. That was the incentive to proceed with a total rehabilitation of the historic structure.

Through a competitive bidding process, Steven and I purchased the vacant St. Louis Board of Education Office Building in 2002. In 2004 our renovations produced 47 loft apartments and first floor commercial space for a restaurant and shops. This is adding substantially to the vital elements of modern and convenient housing in the City's downtown redevelopment. This venture, christened Roberts Lofts on the Plaza, is a key development in downtown St. Louis.

Once we became a stakeholder in downtown St. Louis, we decided to become very aggressive in expanding our downtown ownership portfolio. A member of my staff presented a newspaper article to me. It told of its owner, the Wyndham International, desiring to sell off the Mayfair Hotel.

This hotel was located one block from our lofts project. My thoughts were running wild and I wanted us to move quickly on getting this property under contract. If we bought this beautiful suites hotel, next to St. Louis' convention center, what would we do with it? I thought if it didn't work as a hotel, our exit strategy would be to turn it into lofts. Again I perceived this deal as opportunistic and meeting the rules of real estate.

Owning a convention center hotel was intriguing. We rapidly put together a due diligence team. We boarded the team on our corporate Gulfstream III jet and flew off to Dallas, home of Wyndham International. I brought along my twins, Michael and Jeanne, who where in law school at the time. It is never too early to introduce your children to the business. It was great meeting with the Wyndham team. They offered to manage the hotel if we purchased it and to assist us in any way they could. I knew we did not have the bench strength to operate a hotel. We resisted committing management of the hotel to Wyndham until the price was finalized.

Relationship building can reap tremendous benefits....

While at the corporate offices of Wyndham we met Mr. Fred Kleisner, their Chairman and CEO. Fred, Steve and I became fast friends. He was a twin, and I had my twins there. Fred has a corporate mandate to diversify Wyndham business with various racial groups. There had never been an African American owner of a Wyndham Hotel. He was enthusiastic about this prospect and we liked him. Our time with Fred was soon to be shortened by his need to fly off to Washington DC. He had an important meeting scheduled with some of his business' investors. When we learned he was flying commercially, we offered our Gulfstream III to transport him on this trip. This gesture proved to be very helpful in strengthening our relationship with Fred. And, it proved to be rewarding in our final negotiations of the hotel purchase.

I was delighted when during our final negotiation I was able to demonstrate a financial need to reduce our originally signed contract by four hundred thousand dollars ($400,000) and Fred agreed. The Roberts Mayfair Hotel is the first and only African-American owned hotel in downtown St. Louis.

The Roberts Mayfair also represents the first affiliation of an African American owned hotel with Wyndham. This historic hotel opened in downtown St. Louis in 1926 and was acquired by us in July of 2003. One of the St. Louis' most famous boutique hotels, the Roberts Mayfair sits in the center of the convention district. This 18-story 182-room hotel consists primarily of luxury suites, corporate meetings rooms, a bar and restaurant.

Building on success......

Historically, until the late 1950's, St. Louis was the second largest city in America with high-end theaters. Located next door to the Roberts Mayfair Hotel is an historic and unique entertainment venue known originally as the Orpheum Theater, later named the American Theater. This theater opened in 1917 as a venue for vaudeville shows. Decorated in a lavishly ornamented beaux-arts style, it remained in the original owner's family until purchased by us in December 2003.

Our strategy was to acquire this property to serve as a support location for banquets and corporate events booked at my hotel. With a concert and theater seating capacity of fifteen hundred, it will offer midsize touring shows as well as the non-ticketed special events.

The Roberts Orpheum Theatre is the only remaining eloquent theater in downtown St. Louis.

A unique note on both the Mayfair Hotel and the Orpheum Theater speaks to the change of the times and importance of taking Action. Upon the opening of both these buildings and for decades to follow, African Americans were excluded from lodging at the hotel and viewing performances at the theater. Today, ancestors of the very people discriminated against then, are now the owners of both facilities and are branded by their name!

Chapter 14

LEADERSHIP AND VISION

An Actionaire provides leadership. Leadership is the capability to persuade and influence individuals to perform as directed. Many theories and beliefs offer speculations on the principal qualities of an influential leader. Is it charm and charisma, or deceit and manipulation? Being an effective leader appears to be difficult to define because it is truly an illusive task encapsulated by its own complex nature. One may find it complicated to distinguish a true leader from one who merely offers leadership potential.

The leader is a specific person designated, by some form of bureaucratic process, to direct the operations of an organization. Some individuals accept the responsibility and accountability that accompanies their position. They may function in that position without ever demonstrating leadership. Frequently, we observe a CEO of a company or an elected official holding their respected positions for years without ever advocating change to advance their company or constituents in new directions.

A true leader demonstrates competent leadership abilities. In order to be a leader, the Actionaire must have followers. Merely having subordinates, who are not devotees or supporters, does not make you a leader. In this case, you are a manager. A leader pursues their direction and inspires others to tag along. Basically, the Actionaire leads by setting an example. The Actionaire inspires others' confidence and influences them to follow a mutual effort or calling. In order to succeed in this power of persuasion, the Actionaire must be a confident governor when leading.

Leaders are created through providential moments in time. Our world is filled with individuals who are managers and followers. The Actionaire becomes a leader by initially being a victim of his circumstances. At a given moment and under extraordinary circumstances, they realize their calling. When their leadership abilities surface, they use them to subsequently inspire the confidence and trust of others. The Actionaire responds to his calling, destiny, and responsibility to lead others to their purpose in life. By inspiring others to achieve their purpose, the Actionaire is benefited also. It is possible that the followers' purpose is to be the best managers and workers in the Actionaire's company. By inspiring them to be the greatest managers and workers, the company will in turn release the most beneficial product to humanity.

The Actionaire knows that mankind is taught the importance of following a leader. They understand that without some form of governance, rebellion and disobedience would ensue. To avoid a chaotic society, mankind must be held accountable to one another. This hierarchal system is accomplished through subjection to wealth or authority. The result leads to the relationship of manager and the managed, director and the directed, the master and the servant, the leader and the follower, and the Actionaire and the inert.

The Actionaire is created to lead. They are not a copy; rather, they are the originals. Knowing your calling or your purpose helps you understand and develop the leadership skills within you. Therefore, leadership is synonymous with you knowing and becoming yourself. Some individuals become mired in their social context. They lack the confidence to change and declare independence from the opinions of others. They copy the behavior of their surroundings and are never free to expose their inner leadership qualities.

Leading is simpler than most people think. If you can just naturally be you and learn more about yourself, then your capacity to lead will surface. Learning the advantages of your strengths and weaknesses will enable you to understand yourself and reach success in your life. An Actionaire knows what they want, why they want it, and how to communicate it to others. Their goals are achievable through this knowledge. Their leadership surfaces when they respond to their calling and vision for their lives.

There is no compromising when focused on fulfilling life's goals. This command may be lying deep within you and buried by the misconception that only unique humans attain lofty positions of leadership. There is a leader in each of us. If you enhance your self esteem and change your concept of leadership, then you will find your potential to lead.

Leadership is the ability to sway others by influence. Actionaires uphold the principle that all activities require some level of leadership. It does not mean only directing a corporation or being elected to office. This principle can refer to your influence over your parents, child, neighbor, spouse, gardener, or taxi driver. Actionaires can also be seen simply as responding to responsibility. If you are given responsibility of any measure, you should demonstrate leadership. If you are painting your room, driving people to a sports event, working on your job, or speaking to your children, then you are exercising some measurement of leadership talents.

Leaders are not born. Leaders are created through the dynamics of human experiences. The concept that some are born to lead and others are born to follow is not the opinion of the Actionaire. Leadership is not a product of divine endowment and personality traits as proffered by Plato, Aristotle, and Socrates. The essence of their philosophy has resulted in the historical worldly position that the masses are ruled by a significant few, who are chosen by providence to govern.

Case after case of emerging Actionaires has proven the philosophers' theory to be invalid. Time after time, we have witnessed Royals of countries fail in their governance and lead their countries to disaster. Wealthy heirs with no vision or leadership skills have lost great fortunes. True leaders are not born. True leaders are made. Leaders are made through perseverance and determination. They are sometimes made by accident or through an unusual occurrence in their lives. You cannot learn leadership through a motivational speaker or college course. You cannot be taught character or vision. Leaders are made through developing character and vision. Taking Action can only develop these skills.

The Actionaire understands that their potential must be developed. They possess a guiding vision. They are able to see beyond the mere physical surface. They can see what's down the road and plan the course to reach their destination. This vision may be defined as foresight. Some individuals could have foresight, but fail to tap into insight or their intuition. Actionaires do not accept the minimal state of things; rather, they are interested in the transpiration of events, and their place in advancing the Action. Other people will go with the flow, but the Actionaire creates their own flow. These visionaries are sometimes perceived as oddities. This criticism never stops the Actionaire. Allow yourself to enjoy the visions of the future more than the history of the past. Harboring on the past inhibits you from operating in the present, thereby barring you from advancing your vision.

Without a leader possessing a vision, your company, social club, and community may perish. The Actionaire must have a vision. It imparts challenge and adventure to your life. In our present organizations, we are taught to wait our turn, don't rock the boat, and stay the course. A vision with Action makes a visionary. Action without a vision is a waste.

Some people may have visions without the will to bring them into reality. They dream, but never wake up. Many people share their wonderful concepts with friends and company associates, but ultimately, their concepts continue to reside in their minds due to a lack of Action. You may often hear someone say, "I thought of that (a now money making idea brought into fruition by someone else) years ago."

The Actionaire puts their vision to work. It becomes their mission. It results in their acquisition of wealth and authority.

The Actionaire makes the seemingly impossible become possible. When you have enjoyed those possibilities, it is very difficult to accept the notion of impossibilities.

A vision is a quick view of the possibility. It is a glimpse of your purpose in life. Vision is a representation of the completed efforts that you will soon undertake. The Actionaire understands that vision is the source of restraint and self-indulgence.

Most individuals go though life with no idea of where they will end up. The best solution is to take a few moments and write down your goals in life. This step alone will help you to accomplish more. A goal and a plan will give you direction and a sense of purpose. Everyone is seeking a route to follow in the journey of life.

The Actionaire is ever vigilant and conscious of their glance at destiny. They succeed by indulging their vision.

Chapter 15

BREAKING BARRIERS

An Actionaire is a good conversationalist. Statistically, one of the greatest fears that people have in our society is public speaking. The second greatest apprehension is initializing a conversation with a new person.

The Actionaire knows that most people are shy and uncomfortable starting conversations with strangers. The Actionaire uses this knowledge to gain total control over the direction of any conversation. Some people face the never-ending challenge of communication barriers. They prefer listening to talking. The Actionaire must allow others the occasion to chat by asking for their thoughts and opinions. Knowing how to ask clever questions gives the Actionaire an advantage in most situations.

Through conversation, the Actionaire can reduce anxiety, create cooperation, persuade, and motivate people. If you want to pursue someone, you will progress faster by asking questions than by making a statement. The Actionaire's questions result in acquiring usable information. Some of this information may be used to the detriment of the answering party, while advancing the goals of the Actionaire. This type of misleading behavior is displayed throughout the American corporate and political environment.

Corporate America's management departments and clever political leaders incorporate the use of intelligent inquiries into their system of promotions. The use of the answer is targeted toward the Actionaire's personal mission to gain authority. The Actionaire needs sharp, gifted followers to support their overall mission.

The most obvious purpose of probing is to gather data. Being well informed is essential to achieving success in any scenario. The Actionaire acquires and grasps all types of information. Tapping all sources of information is key to their objective.

Mining for information requires many skills. The Actionaire is careful to not dictate to unsuspecting individuals; rather they give guidance to them in the form of a question. You might ask the question at a corporate meeting; which business plan would best be incorporated into our company's future? Once they have expressed their ideas, the Actionaire then gives them credit for it and

proceeds to adopt the best ideas into their plan. Unfortunately, the corporate and political culture only rewards the Actionaire who takes full credit for the plan. The other individuals, who helped in the formation of the plan, are again manipulated into believing that their ideas will be credited to them in the future. In the end, they continue to find no personal satisfaction or promotion.

Without the comfortable ease of conducting conversation or asking questions, most people remain stuck in a job that never offers them the chance to fulfill their calling. This phobia prevents them from discovering new business opportunities, forging new friendships, and influencing people. They are afraid of voicing opinions that may appear sophomoric or silly. This lack of self-confidence derives from a fear of rejection.

How does a person overcome this weakness and become a tactful conversationalist? What do they recognize as the key to change their Action when they feel the weakness of apathetic, passive behavior? How do you start that conversation and keep it going even at the risk of being rejected?

The Actionaire knows that initiating a conversation may lead to opportunities for making new friends, learning something different, or creating an unexpected business venture. The Actionaire builds a network of people exclusively for social and business purposes. They take the risk of opening the conversation and are adept at relaxing their new friend. Most baby boomers in the United States were raised with the "Leave It to Beaver" mentality. Leave It to Beaver was the family television show that set the standard in parenting.

Other shows of that era, such as Father Knows Best and the Ozzie and Harriet Show, fostered the same values and rules of behavior. Children and parents alike watched these shows religiously.

Parents consistently promoted this "ideal behavior" in their home. These rules of behavior still govern the lives of people today, and these similar rules on conversation are also still taught in most homes. The following rules govern the behavior of some individuals: silence is golden, speak only when spoken to, be seen but not heard, silence is a virtue, be quiet and sit down, wait to be introduced, and good things happen to those who wait.

We were taught this "storybook perfect behavior" in school, on our jobs, and at home. However, we do not learn conversational skills in any institutionalized setting. Do you remember this one growing up, "don't talk to strangers?"

The Actionaire understands how to "break the ice," make it through a silent moment after meeting someone, and avoid awkward dialogue. In order to develop business and political ties, they use diplomatic, direct techniques that break through conversation barriers.

The Actionaire seizes the risk of approaching people and engaging them in conversation. They undertake the responsibility of advancing the conversation toward their objective. Their goal is to establish a level of comfort with the other person. The Actionaire learns early that the first step to a successful conversation is being a good listener and asking the right questions.

A favorite phrase by the Actionaire is, "for our friends we will do anything and for our enemies we follow the law." Making friends in business and politics occurs through conversation. In politics, the Actionaire is known for saying, "I have friends on one side of the issue and friends on the other side of the issue, and first and foremost I support my friends". People always prefer to do business with their friends. The Actionaire begins and ends every business discussion with light, non-business, or friendly conversation.

So how do you not enter into dead end questions? Showing

interest in the opposite party prevents dead end questions. The more interest you show the more interesting you become to them. When you are in a conference room with clients and you exhibit charisma or candid behavior with them, you will be seen as committed to the cause of that client. If you have a certain level of intimacy with your superiors, then they will especially take notice and judge your performance as being of greater value. Your goal is for them to believe that you are a necessary asset to their company or political livelihood. This interpersonal foundation will advance your career or business.

The Actionaire does not wait for others to approach them. They introduce themselves at parties and meetings. They ask questions that are open-ended and answerable:

- How are things at work?
- How is your family?
- What are your views on what happened?
- Who do you think has the best chance of winning (a given political race)?

The key to a successful conversation is to show interest in the other person:

- How did you become interested in starting your business?
- How did you hear about this type of operation?
- What got you involved?
- What are your future plans?
- How will you expand?

- How did you pull it off?
- What were the challenges of starting this fascinating business or political career?
- Did you have any hesitation about starting?
- What are the necessary skills to operate your business?

The Actionaire avoids the dead end questions. When you show interest in someone, they believe that you are concerned about their well-being. This form of sincerity establishes a human connection and serves as building blocks for a successful personal and business relationship. The Actionaire makes it a rule to begin and end every conversation with a brief chat regarding that person's life. If you never connect with others, then you will never know the origin of your next client or business relationship. The rule of thumb is to show interest in everyone and believe that every conversation is an opportunity. If you don't perpetuate this type of behavior, then you may never meet your next friend or key business prospect. Everyone has challenges in their life. In order to succeed, you must accept and overcome this fact.

The Actionaire generates conversation and breaks barriers by approaching people with open-ended and targeted questions. You should exhibit this method of effectual Action in every aspect of your life.

A PERSONAL ANECDOTE

On Being A Tactful Conversationalist......

While in Santa Barbara California, I attended a private wealth management conference for high net-worth African Americans. For several days, I was surrounded by people, who, not unlike this author, were or appeared to be, of substantial means by adorning their accoutrements of wealth: Presidential his and hers Rolexes, or the occasional diamond studded Pâtèk Philippe; the men in their custom monogrammed shirts worn under Oxford, Armani, or Kiton suits; and the women in their newest Escada, Dior or St. John's fashions.

As in the past, when attending similar gatherings, I drew upon my well-honed political instincts for small conversation. The mission is to meet as many people as I can.

This was the last morning of the conference. I served as a speaker on two of the "managing wealth" panels. The result of this exposure afforded me the opportunity to embrace a small degree of celebrity among my fellow attendees.

On the final morning of the symposium, I entered the posh dining area of the Bacara Resort and Spa. After greeting the many new acquaintances developed over those past few days, I sat at a table with a family of three. This was one family with whom I had not linked. They seemed curiously interested in talking with me.

This family was not dressed in the couture of the others, nor were they networking like the other attendees. They were quiet almost shy, or otherwise engrossed in private family chatter. I opened with a few pleasantries and then asked the proverbial question. "What is your line of business?"

The family was comprised of a man in his late forties sporting a 1970's style Afro, his wife, a quite conservative dresser, and their college-age daughter. The father spoke to me about setting up "a couple of car service centers and that he wanted to study the best way to initiate his dream." He paid me a compliment. They indicated that they had spoken to others about me and that I was considered a successful businessman with a chain of accomplished enterprises. They were of the impression I might be able to offer them the type of personal guidance, not made available or offered by others, at the conference.

Our small talk allowed me to build a level of confidence with the family. A barrier was broken and a connection was formed that bestowed a level of comfort with me. Knowing nothing of their background, I proceeded to give them some friendly advice and counsel. I directed the father to other sources for assistance and tendered my telephone number to him for future reference. I spoke with his wife about how she planned to work with him as a team. Their daughter shared her future plans and career goals. As we ended the breakfast, handshakes and hugs were exchanged. They expressed genuine appreciation for the time I spent with them and my open willingness to help them think through their small business startup.

The father, offered another special thanks to me, and then revealed some extraordinary news. The reason he wanted to start this particular business was because he had no other ideas on how to invest the $45 million that he had recently won in the lottery.

Chapter 16

TRANSACTING BUSINESS

The Actionaire negotiates transactions on a daily basis. Negotiations are a major aspect of life. The art of negotiation is illustrated through purchasing furniture, controlling the television remote, hiring an employee, asking for a raise, or deciding on who washes the dishes. The Actionaire attempts to win the best deal possible. The Actionaire does not view negotiations as stressful, agonizing, or frightening.

Most people avoid these types of encounters. The Actionaire sees transactions and negotiations as fun, positive experiences for both involved parties.

It is fun to be creative. It is exciting to give birth to new ideas, places, and businesses. Actionaires are champions at completing their endeavors. They are follow-through people who finish and close every deal.

An Actionaire applies a clear, skilled, systematic approach to their negotiations. They utilize proven strategies. Achieving your requests doesn't mean you can't meet the needs of the other person. Negotiating effectively can lower an interest rate, reduce the purchase price of a car or home, create value in a business, or save you from washing the dishes during Monday Night Football or the Oprah Show.

What is a negotiation? It is working jointly with another person or their representatives to achieve agreeable and mutually acceptable conclusions. The rules are straightforward. Never underestimate your opponent and never accept his first offer.

The first rule is to make certain that the other person believes you respect them. They should not feel threatened during the negotiations. The Actionaire's role is to create the impression that both parties will profit from the deal. Both parties must compromise, while remaining true to the art of negotiation. Bargaining in good faith is the key to the Actionaire's success. The discovery of the other party's reason for negotiating gives the Actionaire a triumphant edge. The Actionaire blatantly states their desire in order to make the other party non-speculative as to their intentions.

The second rule is to understand that every negotiation has at least two or more stances. The skilled Actionaire must understand their position and that of the other party. If you cripple this vital negotiation, you may in fact cause damage to yourself. Knowing the deal in its entirety makes the outcome more plausible for the long term. Evaluating the deal from both sides is not only a matter of fair play, but it is the correct approach for ultimate success.

The third rule is the Actionaire's greatest weapon. The Actionaire must pinpoint the needs and desire of the opposite party. Don't let their stated position govern your Actions and strategy. Targeting your objectives as well as the welfare of the opposite party is the focus of the Actionaire. They construct solutions that achieve the desires of both parties. To mastermind a successful deal, the Actionaire works out creative solutions. Their critical point climaxes when they resolve the vital needs of all parties.

To negotiate effectively, the Actionaire applies certain effective stratagem. They begin with conducting research on the transaction and the rival parties. Preparation is fundamental to your success in the negotiation method. The Actionaire approaches carefully. They do the necessary underpinning study and continue to deliberate on it throughout the process. The preparation process is the most productive stage of a negotiation. The Actionaire constantly explores new ideas and creates inquiries. Within their strategic plans, they determine and introduce the four levels of indulgence.

Inquiring

What will you ask for?

What will you take?

What will be unacceptable?

What is the retreat strategy that permits the door to stay open?

To achieve a successful transaction, the Actionaire must be willing to compromise and make concessions. In preparation for the negotiation, you need to practice different scenarios of your discussions.

Your investigation will prepare you for any response during the bargaining procedure. For example, a used car dealer insists that his price of a pre-owned car is at market value. Your review of the Blue Book for auto price estimates or studying the Internet on used cars comparisons may expose his quote to be $1,500 higher than the market value. By asking him to double-check the market prices, you can now drive his asking price down to a level more suitable to your price goal. There are other key questions that will help you decrease the price. Has the car been in an accident, hailstorm, or flood? Has it been repainted? How many owners has it had? Did a smoker own it? Do you have the automobile's service records?

The time to suggest a lower price becomes a compromise of your own. The Actionaire never appears desperate throughout the negotiation. They can always walk away from a deal. Thoroughly researching your deal will give you the ability to be quick-witted during this intense process. If the opposing party is not a patient person, then you will probably win with any deal you propose, especially when they display ignorance or desperation to finish. The impatient individual never has a plan Beta as back up to the possible failure of plan Alpha. The Actionaire always has a second plan. They know their own desires and breaking point of compromise before they initiate the parley. The greater the deal the more they prepare, and the greater the intensity the more they fine-tune their message.

Agreeing on the Objective

It is important that all parties agree on mutually acceptable objective standards at the outset of the negotiation. What are the ground rules? What is the objective criteria by which all parties can agree?

The objective criteria sets the standard on which a judgment or decision can be based. All parties must be prepared to effectively and clearly communicate their objectives in ways that both will understand. This procedure may take a while, but in the end, it will save time and provide clarity to the deal.

Objective criteria will fund a means of reaching conclusions expeditiously and weed out those unfocused individuals. Finally, all parties must seek mutually supportable positions on both sides. At the end of the negotiation, parties must agree in writing by signing on the final terms. If you don't understand or feel indecisive in regard to the terms of the final agreement, you must seek counsel from an advisor, a business broker, an accountant, and/or an attorney.

In the battle of negotiation, the techniques of an Actionaire are varied and unique; however, there are certain tactics that work with a high degree of success. These tactics will enable you to summarize the concerns or issues of both parties. In the end, you will save time and finalize a deal. A deal maker plays the games taught to you earlier in this book. During negotiations, one must watch for the tricks as well as the tactics.

Grimacing

The grimace is a ploy that is often used by the Actionaire. We have all seen it at one time or another. It is when you receive the first offer by the opposing party and you close your eyes tightly, wink a few times, and show an expression of disapproval. This flinch reaction concludes that you have just experienced an overt, negative reaction to the offer. It informs the other person that you have limits and are not pleased with their opening proposal. This reaction infers that you are refusing this first offer. Nearly every time you are in a first offer situation, you should assume that you could do better. The initial offer should never be accepted. These offers are virtually never firm; therefore, there is always room for a counter offer.

Silence

Silence powerfully counteracts any unpleasing offer. If you don't like what the opponent has said or you are waiting for a response to your offer, silence will work for you. Most people cannot handle dead air time. They frequently become uncomfortable when the quiet void persists. With patience, the Actionaire knows that people will begin to negotiate against themselves. The skilled Actionaire looks for other tactics presented to them. One such tactic is the Good Guy/ Bad Guy routine.

The Actionaire watches for this maneuver and may play along with it at the beginning of the negotiations. They keep their distance from the "good guy" who pretends to be their friend, while suggesting negotiation terms that would be in the best interest of both parties. In fact, the only way the "good guy" benefits is if the deal is consummated at any cost.

It is difficult to negotiate with more than one party. In order to successfully make a deal, the Actionaire realizes that they need access to all parties in the negotiation. Let's keep in mind that these are in fact the tactics used by the Actionaire as an authority play to win the negotiations. The strategic negotiator resists these techniques by playing along with them and not ignoring them. If the "good guy" pushed too hard, then inform him that you know his interest is in making the deal happen and not in protecting you.

Negotiations are a series of offers and counter offers. The most appropriate phrase to apply here is "keep the ball in their court." Have them make the first offer. Ask them to give you their option on the value of the item or company to be acquired. This maneuver helps the Actionaire understand the other party's interest. You will find out how rigid or flexible the other party is in the deal.

Probing

The Actionaire frequently asks questions to measure up his target. Have you ever considered barter arrangements for your car? If I paid cash today, how much would you charge? If I purchased more than one, how would you feel about unloading them for a deep discount? These questions are not real offers; they help you delve into the mindset of the target without making a firm offer. The target is then positioned to respond. The correct answer is not to answer. If the opposing party is an Actionaire, then they will respond by asking a follow up question.

How would this barter arrangement work? How much cash are you considering to offer? How many would you be interested in purchasing? These questions tell you that they are setting you up. The Actionaire forces the other person into making the first move or the first offer.

Positioning

A popular tactic in a negotiation is taking the position of one who cannot make the decision alone. This strategy always gives you the out to "take the offer back to the other parties." This ruse buys time and gives you a bargaining tool. You may hear the other person state, "I don't think he will take this offer, but I will take it back and see."

You should always position yourself with the decision maker or the one with the authority to make the deal. When you are face to face with the decision maker, you can begin real negotiations. You can, in good faith, begin to find compromises to achieve your goal. Remember you are only comfortable making concessions as long as you are receiving them in return. Trade offs are relevant to a successful negotiation. If both parties have a reasonable attitude toward the negotiation, then they will each succeed. They should discuss their feelings openly and cooperate with each other.

Site Selection

Your meeting location will give you an advantage and disadvantage. If you are on your playing field, you will feel more comfortable. If you are on their home ground, they cannot use the strategy of checking with their higher ups before a decision can be made. If parties cannot agree on either one of their locations, then a neutral location must be determined.

Closing the Transaction

A helpful hint is to set an agenda. An agenda outlines the goals of the negotiation. Parties need to agree on the facts of the deal in order to begin negotiations in earnest. What are your negotiations about?

The Actionaire learns the needs or desires of the other person. Once both sides understand the facts, then they will gain joint satisfaction. To reach an agenda that is meaningful, the Actionaire will ask questions to understand the other party.

The Actionaire watches the body language of the other party. Their words may suggest a friendly position while their non-verbal expressions may show a completely different position. Observing a person's behavior and physical posture is very important. Frequently, body language represents people's feelings. By watching the body language, the Actionaire can understand the energy that he created

with the other person. If the other party's body language reeks of discomfort, then you may be creating a negative attitude toward the deal. This negative energy may cause major problems and disrupt the negotiations. The Actionaire knows that it is important to observe this body language and change your course of Action before it negatively impacts the deal. Keep a close watch on the other party.

A simple understanding of one's approach to negotiating is to know the fundamentals of strategizing and tactical actions. The strategy is your long-term plan and the tactics are your short-term Actions. This information makes the Actionaire more confident, effective, and successful in every aspect of their life.

Preparation allows you to learn about the target items for which you bargain. The Actionaire negotiates by knowing the factual elements of the arrangement and planning the route to meet the challenge. Making reasonable requests or demands in the deal avoids total rejections or emotional exaggerations. You reach the facts through verification and research, but not through assumptions. The result is to know the other person's needs inside the arrangement. In sum, mutual satisfaction creates a good negotiation and rapidly brings closure to the transaction.

Chapter 17

FINAL THOUGHTS

The Actionaire recognizes their life's purposes by listening to the voice of their heart and mind. Since birth, personal opinions, ideas, and prophecy have directed their mission and passion.

However, at various points in time, distracters will attempt to deter you from your purpose. There will be efforts by others to manipulate you and people may falsely accuse you. Without control of your response to these and other distractions, you will experience destruction. Reacting angrily and seeking revenge will lead to bad decisions and regrets. If you are slow to anger, you will be fast to greatness.

The Actionaire trains their inner spirit to say no to their adversary and rebuffs feelings of resentment and rivalry. Your adversary may be a close associate or even a family member. They will attempt to drain you of resources under the cloak of need. If you are to grow your financial base and personal strength, you must learn the strength of a decline. A simple NO, directed to those people focused on exploiting your giving characteristics, is authoritative and commanding. Some, in your family, friendship pool, or the general populace, seem to be exceptionally professional at requesting or soliciting money and favors from you. They want to borrow your car, notwithstanding their failure to have auto insurance; or, they badger you to temporarily live at your home "for yet a couple of days," which turns into a departure date filled with ambiguity. When you decline them you can discover their true motive. Watch their reaction to you, when you say NO. There are people in your life today who are of the remarkable opinion that when you get a job or your business succeeds, it is "their blessing." They create justifications and seductions to tap into your assets with total disregard.

An Actionaire evaluates their personal relationship with people and puts them in perspective with their goals. "A parasite wants to take what your have earned but a partner desires to obtain what you have learned."

When climbing the ladder of success you will encounter resentful and envious people.

The Actionaire Does It Anyway!

When you demonstrate leadership, people will loathe you.

The Actionaire Does It Anyway!

When you exhibit enjoyment of life, people will resent you.

The Actionaire Does It Anyway!

When you express your beliefs, people will disagree with you.

The Actionaire Does It Anyway!

When you take Action, people will disparage and criticize you.

The Actionaire Does It Anyway!

Why does the Actionaire do it anyway? In the end, your Actions are between you and your spiritual maker; therefore, it is no one's concern.

If you are unclear as to your purpose, then you must seek out the deepest desires within you. In order to recognize your purpose and mission, you must differentiate between your true desires and your passing interests. You could have an interest in one function, but not have a passion to pursue it. If you discover your passion and actively pursue your vision, then events will transpire bringing it to fruition. Remember that one person with a vision is greater than hundreds of passive seekers who live by minimal standards.

The relentless pursuit of your dreams, regardless of great obstacles, identifies your true purpose. When people think "Oh no, that's impossible for me to do", they settle for less and remain unfulfilled.

The only time people have limits or boundaries is when they formulate them.

Shakespeare once said, "Nothing is either good or bad, only thinking makes it so."

The idea that nature makes no judgment on behavior, only people do, is a profound thought when you face a daily barrage of ethical questions and status quo dogma. We live in a world of judgmental people. Notwithstanding our willingness to distinguish good and bad as being one of our most enhancing attributes, it is vitally important to realize that "good" and "bad" are categories imposed on the world and not of the world per se.

In business the Actionaire measures risks and pursues their calling, vision and mission without the **fear of failure**. What would your life be like if you could eliminate the **fear of failure?** How different would you be today? Fear is a concept formed in your mind, it is not a physical impediment or barrier. Failure is only a representation of an unexpected or non-preferred outcome. This experience should merely be considered a learning event.

Many people live their life reliving memories of failure. They spend hours lamenting and considering their collapse, doubts or misgivings. The Actionaire lives with imagination, vision and dreams. They only consider the future while fulfilling the present. The Actionaire has no **fear of failure**, as failure is only a mental enigma or aberration. An appropriate analogy is found in driving a car. It is impossible to drive an automobile by looking only in the rear view mirror. In order for one to successfully drive, looking forward through the front glass is mandatory. The Actionaire is focused on the present and seldom looks backward. The Actionaire recognizes the complexity between the physical and conceptual. This may bring about great confusion to some people. Theoretical reality is formulated in the mind. It is then spoken or written in a theme, which makes it seem accurate, although it is a construct.

Our spoken word is replete with concepts that have no existence in the physical; no time and space reference. However, they seem as real as anything tangibly or physically held by you. For example impartiality, ethics, or moral principles are concepts we have established to meet the human objectives that nature does not encompass. This is our method of assessing each other's performance. Consider all words and concepts are only made up by people and are not matter created by nature. Words create half formed ideas, merely notions or simply inventions expressed though verbal communication.

If you experience misdirection on a business deal, lose a property acquisition, or have a personal downside, be careful finding comfort in rationalizing through words like, "I guess it was not meant to be." If a young person dies accidentally or even after an extended illness, they will say, "Well, I guess it was his time."

If a person believes he or she has bad luck when it comes to succeeding in business, primarily because every time they try they fail, they reach the outrageous conclusion that it is their destiny not to be in business. So they assume that this is a permanent condition and live a lifetime of constraint.

These types of people accept the belief that they are in an irreversible descending freefall; they assume the world has placed this burden on them and that is the way things are in life. They exist far from the truth. In fact, life would be substantially different if they changed their perspective.

Have you ever stated that you think outside the box? What a non-descript concept! This statement "**thinking outside the box**" begs the question, are you in a box? Doesn't it make the assumption or inference that you are in a box? Now, my request to you is to offer yourself an explanation or definition of your box. What is the size of your box? Is it the size of an auditorium, a prison cell, or a casket? I have a little secret for you and it's good news...there is no box, only the horizon. An Actionaire horizonist is one who is free of stereotypes, psychological shackles, mental blocks, limitation of thought and **"in the box"** lifestyle. The Actionaire is a no box thinker. They are forward thinking horizonists; pursuing their dreams with bravado, embracing no limitations or verbal hyperbole.

Dreams and aspirations will not necessarily make you financially wealthy; however, everyone should take time to figure out what their dreams and aspirations are. Some have not done this yet, but it's time. The Actionaire understands that dreams and aspirations come directly from your spirituality, listen to that inner voice. Trusting our instincts will release every healthy human being's power to make choices and pursue the opportunities. This will assist you in earning your destiny.

It is up to you to select what those choices will be. Why not choose to make money? It is not a sin to have money, or know how to make money. The Actionaire makes money and shares that knowledge with others. This builds the Actionaire's legacy.

Becoming an Actionaire formulates an attitude that will introduce you to new and untapped opportunities. Business deals are sitting dormant awaiting your embrace. This is the opposite view held by those who think there is a short supply of potential investments or they have convinced themselves that they simply have bad business karma. Unfortunately they have not explored the passion and vision within them, which will provide guidance and confidence needed to discover the tools necessary to embark upon a life of wealth and authority.

Actual scarcity of potential businesses is not the same as a scarcity opinion. In a community with limited numbers of resources, such as on a small isolated island, one could determine that an actual scarcity of goods or resources exists. However, that is not the same as a scarcity opinion, which is an attitude prevailing in some people. This scarcity opinion is an attitude, which is the undiscriminating, ongoing belief that life offers very few business opportunities and that you must plant all your energy into working for someone else. The feeling that the supply of certain types of business opportunities are fixed, limited and may eventually run out, is the attitude that prompts people to treat others as competitors. This concern surfaces regardless of the probability another person could successfully capture their opportunities.

On the whole, opportunities are likely to come to you in greater abundance when you show confidence and passion for business deals. A business deal is your invention and you control its possibilities.

Passive people allow the conceptual to control the physical. Your life can be as complex as you make it, just remain grounded in the belief that judgmental thinking should be checked for reality and not be taken as fact. After all, it is only conceptuality. Nature renders no verdict. People perform that task.

The world is counting on you to open up the potential within you and discover what you are capable of achieving.

Our society has trained and brainwashed people to dream small, think trivially, expect the insignificant, and not do anything too major. When we compare society's rules of behavior with our actual dreams, our purpose appears unrealistic and insignificant.

In order to accept, pursue and achieve your purpose fully,

you will have to develop persistence and self-discipline. Persistence and self-discipline require Action, and Action will occur within the limits of time.

Time is everything to the Actionaire. Time is a measurement of existence. Time is available to everyone. The rich and the poor have access to the same amount of time. Everyone should manage his or her time well. We must be decisive and disciplined in how we spend our time, with whom we share our time, what we create with our time, and where we choose to exist within our time.

Time is the Actionaire's greatest asset. It must be used wisely. Clever slogans, such as "time waits for no one," "now is the time", "time is of the essence", "time is running out" "time kills deals" and "this is our time", extol the point that time only exists in the now. One must act in the now to achieve the gifts of the future.

Every morning each of us is presented with the gift of 86,400 seconds to utilize. Conceptualize it as if you are holding an account in a bank and everyday that balance must be spent. This holding balance sustains no accruing interest and it must be depleted daily. With this account you either "use it or you lose it". Everyday, every second in your life must be used in an achieving way. The Actionaire does not say, "have a nice day," instead they say "HAVE AN ACHIEVING DAY."

How will you take advantage of this gift of time? You have only the seconds in this given time period to act. That is nature's gift to you. You must understand that each moment expires even as you think of it. The old existentialist once stated "you can never step in the same river once." This expression underlines the belief that change is constant and all you have is the now.

Therefore, Action has no other time than the present and that is why ACTION HAS NO SEASON.

Reader Commentary & Book Reviews

Here's what others have said after reading Michael Roberts' groundbreaking philosophy............

"Thoroughly enjoyed your new book and found it quite inspirational. One year I gave How Proust Can Change Your Life to all my friends as a Christmas gift. Next Christmas it will be your book! I loved it."

B. L., 7/28/05 Phoenix, AZ

"Finally a book that actually gives you the formula for success. Understanding Mike Roberts mind-pattern, the mind pattern of an entrepreneurial genius, is truly invaluable! I enjoyed the ride as Mike steered me through the laws of business, man, and nature as he sees it. Hitting on subjects from business strategies that professors won't speak of in school, to the power of positive thinking and self confidence, to tapping into and harvesting the powers of the universe – this is a detailed instruction book on how to align yourself with inevitable success and prosperity. It's about creating and achieving your destiny – working with change not against it, overcoming adversity and thriving on it. This book should be a bible for those on the frontline of human evolution. Be prepared to enter into a new realm of existence and possibility upon reading this book and watch how magnificently life can unfold for you when you do it right! Thank you Mike Roberts for sharing your profound philosophies!

S.W., 6/7/06 Chicago, IL

"I am really enjoying reading your book. I must confess, though, that as I read, I am skipping around, but that doesn't seem to detract from the continuity. I suppose after reading the Forward, Preface, Acknowledgements, Introduction and Chapter I, it doesn't appear to require sequential reading. If I were still serving as an adjunct professor at one of the local colleges/universities, I could very well require that my students read those aforementioned sections as prerequisites, then assign chapters, ongoing, as appropriate. There are gems throughout! You may not agree with this reading order, and I may not either, later. Of course, when I read it again, I will read it straight through and will be able to make a better assessment. " "I am honored to accept the "title" of Actionaire that you bestowed upon me (smile)! As I have been reading, I get another opportunity to reflect on my own achievements. I can see through your eyes, that taking **action** was what propelled a shy little girl with a dream, from a family of 8, who grew up in the South, into a confident, successful woman. "

B. J., 10/2/05 Boston, MA

"I am really enjoying your book. I must say it is encouragement to push for more. I know that I am an "Actionare" and there is nothing else to do but make it happen. "I'm writing you for two reasons, the first is to say a heartfelt, "Thank You"! I recently read your book for the 2nd time. The first time I read it while in the library with my son doing homework, so I read it really fast. I purchased the book after that, because I just couldn't stop thinking about it. And, I wanted to train my mind to think like an Actionaire. "Upon reading the book the 2nd time around, I became even more amazed than the first time. I was able to relate to every aspect of the book, and found myself deeply entwined in your world and what makes you tick. The book is so well written, that it's as if you made a personal appearance in my home to lecture me one on one. Oh my goodness, I can't' put into words, how you've touched my life with this book. (And, I'm a writer). Your book has become the, "blueprint" for my business journey. No way, did I learn any of this in school!"

L.G.R., 4/5/06 Miami, FL

"My book is in terrible shape because the cover is bent out of sort and the pages have many marks and underlines. My rule has always been to never write in books, but, I could not resist, for your words jumped off the pages yelling at me to make notes. So, needless to say I will be purchasing an additional copy to keep on my shelf."

J.D., 8/29/05 Madison, IL

"I have a few favorite quotes from the book that I would like to share with you: 1. "Your residency does not govern your calling". Growing up the product of a single parent home in North

St. Louis, I often told myself that, "where I was did not dictate where I was going", and I constantly preach this point to my cast, and try to relay this to our audiences. 2. "Opportunity will always find your door step if you look only slightly into the future". 3. "Remember that one person with a vision is greater than hundreds of passive seekers who live by minimal standards". Amen, hallelujah that! (Mr. Roberts that one would make a great bumper sticker or bill board)."

E.Y.E., 9/1/05 Ft. Collins, CO

"You should know that I actually have a list of my favorite quotes from the book; a total of 55 to be exact. I speak them out loud each morning after prayer, and this is now the way I start my day. Again, I say thank you! For, sharing and for caring enough to take the time to do this book! I'm thinking about purchasing copies to give to my cast and band!"

S.C., 3/22/06 Washington, DC

"Staci and I have been traveling lately, but we were able to pick up a copy of the book. We immediately engrossed ourselves in your passion for action and real world anecdotes. EM-POWERING and ENLIGHTENING are words that only come close in describing the book's profound impact. I always find myself feverishly trying to remember all the things you have taught me in our short relationship, but the book allows me to really absorb your business savvy/creativity. Thanks for your mentorship and willingness to impart crucial knowledge. Action is power!!!"

R.P., 8/15/05 St. Louis, MO

"I went home and devoured your book, finding it both insightful and well written. It was with great relief that I discovered my own worthiness to be classified as an Actionaire."

S.L.M., 9/26/05 Northlake, IL

"After more than thirty years in business I didn't even know that I was an Actionaire until I met Mike at a business conference. After meeting Mike Roberts and reading his book I immediately became connected to the fact that he is successful because he is so authentic and true to his own calling and vision."

S. M., 7/27/05 Hartford, CT

"Your book give birth to Actionaires, this goes without saying. I like the facts you stated in each chapter, the examples of the business opportunities you have taken. Your book should be in all of our black colleges, thanks again for this book I will share with my colleagues."

L.D., 5/2/06 Las Vegas, NV

"Well, I just finished "Action Has No Season" and I'm left with a new outlook, a new journey and a new vision pertaining to my businesses. Whereas many do not understand my obsession as a business woman, I've watched my visions turn into realities right before my eyes. The most important thing I realized while reading your book is that I carry many traits of being an Actionaire, however, there is still work to be done. Below are only a few, of many, partial quotes from your book that I will take with me on my future journey. Many, I have truly lived by, but others, I still have to filter into my plan.

"You must not only have teammates, but...

"That which happens to you...that which you make happen."

"If you're not working, you're not...

"Opportunity will always find...

"Real success is not a destination, but a journey!!!"

(One of my favorites)

"Not all change creates opportunity...

"Time is the Actionaire's greatest asset."

"True leaders are not born, but they are made."

"Harboring on the past inhibits you from...

"Have an achieving day."

(Brilliant!)

B.M.H., 8/23/05 St. Louis, MO

"I am so eager after reading your book I am gaining authority of my life, I can't wait for November to come, so I can begin my quest into wealth by January 2006 God's willing my position now will be a great story. Thanks for giving me that idea. Now I am taking action."

C.C., 8/8/05 Nassau, BAH

"I read your book "Action Has No Season", and I absolutely loved it! I think it should be required reading for all young adults, (especially African-Americans) before they graduate high school. Had this book been available during the time I attended school. I would have been a different person today, mapping out my life in a more cogent fashion. Being born a person of very limited means from Brooklyn,

Illinois on Christmas Eve, I always believed I was destined for great things being born on the day before the Savior's birth is celebrated had to mean something special. To me, it represented that I was supposed to do something great in my lifetime! {To me} It meant that I would be the designated one in the family to get out and do something good for the less fortunate in my community and the world at large. Having had some success in the broadcast world, I'm still trying to do some good for the world-wide village and your book has given me a greater sense of direction and definitely more confidence in myself and my abilities. I know now that this is my season, and everything that I have gone through has prepared me for **THIS TIME.**"

E.A., 3/29/05 Denver, CO

"Concerning your work, I liked many things about your book but one of the most powerful passages for me was on page 26 paragraph 2:

"The 'Actionaire' is not stalled by the past. Their calling remains true no matter which path they take or past mistakes they have made. The 'Actionaire' remains focused on achieving the intended goal".

Thank you so much for this book. It has meant the world to me..."

G.T., 4/5/06 Los Angeles, CA

"I certainly enjoyed the book. It was a quick read, yet it managed to outline your basic philosophy while proving the credibility of that philosophy with concrete examples. I have never heard the word "Actionaire" before....it must be a Mike Roberts created word.....but I like it because it instantly communicates a concept. As I moved from chapter to chapter, I kept envisioning the Nike swoosh logo and the company's "Just do it" phrase. Your term "Actionaire" brings that to mind. Some other thoughts: Tenacity and determination.....it took you six years to get the license for your television station, so I guess 2 years of seeking a sponsorship for J.R. doesn't seem quite so bad." "Chapter 8 ....the Actionaire's personal and business lives are one.....they challenge the societal rules of separating work and play. I'd never really given that much thought. But I have to agree with your philosophy. We are each one being...to try to divide our approach to life between work and family is a distraction that diminishes our ability to be effective. "I like your positive approach of never saying no to an opportunity...... by looking at everything you certainly increase the possibilities for success. I wish that you would reconsider the opportunity to become involved with J.R. I believe that it will take an African-American with your vision to bring diversity to motorsports. Racing is a pretty tight circle to break into if you are not "connected", and needless to say minorities do not have those connections. I have a sense that you have experienced success in dealing with these kinds of challenges before. "I know that you wrote the book for your children, but I believe that they didn't really need to read it. I'm sure that you have taught them by the way in which you live your life everyday. However, I'm certain that your book will inspire others beyond your family. Thanks for sharing your philosophy. "

P.K., 9/26/05 Indianapolis, IN

"Wow! I just finished reading your book, and I tell you, I had to start over three times reading the preface and the introduction.

Yes, it's a must read and pretty deep if I must say. I know the author is DEEP. It's really interesting because I know you, and I was able to follow some of the family and St. Louis history. What is really interesting is the end results and where you are today. I love the term "Actionaire". Mike this book is one that will assist in keeping one grounded while continuously pointing out the importance of self love, positive self assurance, self confidence, and moving forward with positive self motivation. The "Actionaire ". I have always been one to believe that the world is mine, everyone else just lives in it. People have always said that I was stuck up, self centered, and all the other negative judgments that come with being responsible and taking care of business. Mike I have a totally different outlook on life, now that the girls are older, V.J. is doing well (you would know that), and I am understanding the Real estate industry— "and learning to WORK IT" — They have seen nothing yet . I am so ready to make some REAL MONEY . I have always lived my life "Doing what I wanted to do' at least I thought I was independent. I now have come to realize that Wealth and Authority provides for Real independence. Chapter 6,- Your focal point., Chapter 11,- Summon your Motivation, Chapter 15 - Breaking Barriers ,Chapter 17 - Final Thoughts, Mike this is a great book. I'll use the strategies all the time. Thus far, Fake it till you Make it, I've done pretty good. At this point in my life, Bump Faking any more, I have been very patient, and blessed. Yes there have been hurdles to jump, obstacles to overcome, and big bridges to cross, and I know that there will be many more and some quite difficult. I have no fear because an Actionaire Does it Anyway!"

S.C.J., 7/24/05 Dallas, TX

"My husband, Raphael, and I have been devouring your book. I'm sure he has already expressed our enjoyment of it to you. But, I simply have to take the opportunity to give my compliments as well. In this era when a sense of entitlement seems to trump the sense of initiative. When mindless, easy answers are accepted in lieu of having to deal with complexities. When the grayness of status quo is embraced instead of the vividness of proactive evolution; and above all sloth is accepted instead of action. It was both a refreshment and a pleasure to read a book from a man who walks the walk and who showed no fear in telling the 'in your face' truth about business and the way the world works. This book is an inspiration to all of us who are taking action every moment of every day. Sincere thanks to you for sharing this wisdom with the world."

S. P., 8/5/05 Cleveland, OH

"Mike, I was thrilled to arrive at my office this morning and see that you've sent me a copy of your book! I purchased a copy earlier this week while I was in St. Louis - so now I'll have a copy to share with friends and one to keep and cherish. One of the aspects that I love best about my job is that it allows me the opportunity to meet people like you who are truly inspiring and who are making the world a better place. Thank you - this is an honor. "

S.R., 10/5/05 New York, NY

"I just finished reading your book "Action Has No Season." Thank you, thank you, thank you. I realize the success I have had is because I followed the principals you outline.However, I have to admit that lately I have become a bit complacent (being satisfied with the status quo). Reading your book put me back on track. Now my goal is to live every day as an "Actionaire." Your book will be required reading for my children."

M.D., 12/6/05 Washington, DC

"Michael Roberts boldly takes his readers where other authors refuse to go; into the mind, spirit, and soul of a true achiever. Many authors of "success" books keep it vague, yet he presents concrete, step-by-step, instructions on how to achieve success, based on his personal experiences. He is truly a testament of his words. If the readers of this book read with an open mind, they, too, will find themselves on the threshold of success."

K.M., 3/22/06 Houston, TX

"Finally a book that actually gives you the formula for success. Understanding Mike Roberts mind-pattern, the mind pattern of an entrepreneurial genius, is truly invaluable! I enjoyed the ride as Mike steered me through the laws of business, man, and nature as he sees it. Hitting on subjects from business strategies that professors won't speak of in school, to the power of positive thinking and self confidence, to tapping into and harvesting the powers of the universe- this is a detailed instruction book on how to align yourself with inevitable success and prosperity. It's about creating and achieving your destiny, - working with change not against it, overcoming adversity and thriving on it. This book should be a bible for those on the frontline of human evolution. Be prepared to enter into a new realm of existence and possibility upon reading this book and watch how magnificently life can unfold for you when you do it right! Thank you Mike Roberts for sharing your profound philosophies!"

A.J., 7/28/05 Columbia, SC

"Michael Roberts helps his readers understand the actions, behaviors, and qualities of a true "Actionaire". Readers will be inspired and empowered to assertively take action, thus reaching unimaginable levels of achievement. This book is essential for understanding how internal commitment, discipline, and self-motivation lead to success."

P.J., 4/14/07 Atlanta, GA

"Michael Roberts is a savvy businessman that has taken risks and actions when no one else thought it would be possible for him to achieve. Roberts leads a multi-million dollar, multidimensional conglomerate corporation that exists because he stepped out on faith. He is an ACTIONAIRE - someone that establishes a vision, builds relationships to accomplish tasks, seeks opportunities to serve the community while acting on all reasonable proposals that come his way." "ACTION HAS NO SEASON" offers tools and strategies, which will help you gain wealth and authority. Some of the strategies detailed are: the difference between power and authority; being rich and wealthy; and being a leader and follower. You should understand your motivation for change and be open to taking the steps to master that change by using any means necessary. Clear examples from Roberts career provide inspiration and insight on the Actionaire concept. Roberts does an excellent job at sharing his experiences in business. The concept of the Actionaire works to propel the movement of black entrepreneurship and empowerment. This book is a must read for everybody that wants to create wealth for their family and provide authority to their community. Michael Roberts is to the African American community as Bill Gates is to the computer Industry – everyone should read, understand, and act now! A true Actionaire does not wait for someone else to start the movement they make the movement happen."

M.B., 1/17/06 Oklahoma City, OK

"Michael V. Roberts, J.D. is more than just a successful business man that many individuals can learn from. In his newest book titled, "Action Has No Season", he provides a wealth of vital information that will leave you in awe. In addition, Roberts shares with readers his success story and offers his wisdom and advice as to how you too can gain wealth and authority. Some insights in his book include: shaping your visions, creating your destiny, mastering your emotions, breaking barriers, leadership and much, much more. As a growing business woman, my words can not express how informative this book was to me. I encourage ALL Americans who have the desire to live the American Dream, but have little or no direction, to learn how it can be done through reading, "Action Has No Season." I consider the Roberts brothers as first-class business men whom St. Louis is certainly proud to have as leaders in our community. They have turned our city into one that we all can be proud of for many, many years to come. I do, however, feel the need for many more of us, especially African Americans, to seek for our calling in life. By doing so, it brings about much joy and plenty of happiness. Thanks, Mr. Roberts, for the eye-opening experience and I wish you much more continued success. "

B.H., 8/23/05 St. Louis, MO

"Raw and existential life/business advice from a proven winner! I read this book in two sittings and immediately purchased three additional copies for my closest friends. The author's background and down-to-earth writing style make it easy for young people and entrepreneurs of similar upbringing to relate; motivation is the result! Thank you Mr. Roberts for sharing your strategies and secrets to gaining wealth and authority in our growing global economy."

Dr. J.R., 2/12/06 Minneapolis, MN

ABOUT THE AUTHOR

Chairman/CEO The Roberts Companies

Michael Roberts is the classic American entrepreneur. Born to middle class hard working parents, educated in the St. Louis public school system, he worked his way through college and law school to become one of St. Louis' leading businessmen. Throughout his rise in business, Mr.Roberts maintained a strong commitment to the African-American community from which he came. Locating his headquarters in the heart of this community, his endeavors over the last twenty-nine years have created thousands of jobs and entrepreneurial opportunities, raised the level of economic activity and enhanced the quality of life for the African-American community.

Mr. Roberts' broad range of professional knowledge and experience developed as both a business owner and public official (St. Louis Board of Aldermen, 1977-1985) encompasses the application of innovative financing strategies for large public projects, public-private sector development negotiation strategies, and successful management techniques for urban commercial properties. His leadership in the creation of innovative strategies for financing of redevelopment projects propelled the City into a major redevelopment phase that lasted throughout the 1980s.

Roberts-Roberts & Associates, (RR&A) was founded by Michael Roberts and his brother Steven in 1974. RR&A is a minority-owned business consulting and construction management firm headquartered in St. Louis, MO. RR&A serves major corporations, governmental and quasi-governmental agencies, and private owners in the management of all phases of a construction project, including the design and management of programs to ensure the participation of Minority-owned, Women-owned, and Local Small Businesses. RR&A has served as consultant to a wide variety of public and private sector clients over the past twenty-nine years, managing MBE/WBE participation as construction contractors, vendors and suppliers in projects throughout the country whose cumulative cost exceeds $30 billion.

Roberts Broadcasting Company, was founded in 1989 by Michael and his brother Steve. Roberts Broadcasting [RBC] is licensee for WRBU-TV, Channel 46, in St. Louis, MO, the first African-American owned, full-power television station to enter the St. Louis market in over twenty years. Originally, an affiliate of Home Shopping Network, TV46 became an affiliate of UPN in April 2003. In September of 2006, WRBU will become an affiliate of FOX owned MYNETWORK TV. WRBU broadcasts to over 2.5 million viewers in the St. Louis ADI.

In the early 1990's Roberts Broadcasting began an expansion that added nine full power and two low power minority-owned television stations in:

Denver,CO (Sold)   **Raleigh-Durham**,NC (Sold)
Nashville,TN (Sold)   **Jackson**,MS (Launched 2006)
Hartford,CT (Sold)   **Columbia**,SC (Launched 2006)
Salt Lake City,UT (Merger).**Mobile**,AL low power (Sold)
Albuquerque,NM (Merger) **Pensacola**,FL.low power (Sold)
Evansville, IN (Launched 2007)
Santa Fe,NM (Sold)

Roberts Brothers Properties,was formed in 1982 as Kingsway Centre Partnership when Mr.Roberts purchased the old Sears [department store] building, now named the Victor Roberts Building, which stood vacant in a severely depressed section of St. Louis City. The city's largest commercial office building outside of the downtown business district (200,000 square feet), the old Sears building threatened to become a symbol of the pervasive economic depression that plagued St. Louis' inner-city. By 1985, under Mr. Roberts' business leadership and hard work, the Victor Roberts building had become a thriving commercial center, delivering goods and services to more than 3,000 people per day. Mr. Roberts' success in revitalizing this commercial center was characterized by his ability to create innovative financing strategies and recruit a mix of tenants, which maximized social and economic benefits for the community. In 1991, the Roberts' added significantly to their community's economic progress with the opening of a new Aldi Supermarket -the largest Aldi store in the state of Missouri -constructed on the corner of the building's parking lot. In 1999, Mr.Roberts developed the 14,000 square foot out parcel adjacent to the Victor Roberts Building, attracting Blockbuster Video into the minority community for the first time. This development also includes a Domino's Pizza and State Farm Insurance office.

Roberts Lofts on the Plaza, Roberts Lofts is RBP's major development project in downtown St.Louis. Mr.Roberts purchased the old St.Louis School Board building in 2003. Renovation to provide 47 loft apartments and commercial space on the first floor adds the vital element of modern and convenient housing in the City's downtown redevelopment activities.

Roberts Place, includes renovation of the historic Enright School into 70 apartments and construction of 24 new 3,000 square foot single family homes. The single family homes are designed to meet the LEED (Leadership in Energy & Environmental Design) standards for environmentally sustainable and responsible development. Roberts Place is a gated community with 24/7 on-site security and free broadband Internet access to all apartments and homes.

Roberts Place Groundbreaking June, 2006.

Roberts Centre of Denver, is an office building near the African-American community known as Five Points and only minutes from downtown Denver, CO.

Roberts Wireless Communications –America's

First 100% African-American Owned Digital PCS Telephone Company, Built from the Ground Up

In early 1998, Mr. Roberts initiated discussions with Sprint PCS in Kansas City to explore affiliation opportunities. In June of 1998, Roberts signed an affiliation agreement with Sprint PCS.

As the only Sprint PCS affiliate in Missouri, RWC built and operated a network that provides Sprint PCS service to over 2.5 million residents of Missouri, Illinois and Kansas.

Mr.Roberts' success in financing and building a wireless telephony network in record time led to a merger of Roberts Wireless Communications with Alamosa PCS, Washington-Oregon Wireless, and Southwest PCS in February 2001 creating Sprint PCS's largest affiliate with coverage of over 15 million people in thirteen states. This company was acquired by Sprint-Nextel in February, 2006.

Roberts Tower Company – America's 2ⁿᵈ Largest
Privately Held Tower Company

Roberts Tower Company was formed as a result of Roberts Wireless' merger with Alamosa PCS. Mr.Roberts retained ownership of communications towers in Missouri, Illinois, Kansas, and Oklahoma. With Alamosa (a Sprint PCS affiliate) as the anchor tenant, Roberts Tower Company is growing fast as other service providers such as AT&T, Sprint PCS, Verizon, T-Moblie and Cingular seek tower space in the Midwest. Additionally, it owns and operates television broadcast towers in Missouri, Utah, New Mexico and Tennessee, South Carolina and Mississippi.

Roberts Plaza, LLC was formed in 1999 when Mr.
Roberts purchased a strip shopping center and freestanding grocery store in St.Louis' fashionable central west-end. Anchored by St. Louis' largest grocery store operator, and located at one of the busiest intersections in the city, Roberts Plaza has succeeded in recruiting a new Hollywood Video store and several specialty retailers such as Street Legends and Payless Shoe Store to fill the strip center.

The Shops at Roberts Village, a 42,000 square foot shopping center was completed in early 2003 and brings a new shopping plaza creating new jobs to the area adjacent to the Victor Roberts building. Mr. Roberts received the **Spirit of St. Louis Award,** presented by the Mayor, in recognition of his contribution to the City's revitalization.

Roberts Mayfair Hotel -the first and only African-American owned hotel in downtown St. Louis.

806 St. Charles Street
St. Louis MO 63101
314-421-2500

The Roberts Mayfair also represents the first affiliation of an African-American owned hotel with Wyndham Hotels, Inc. This historic hotel opened in downtown St.Louis in 1926 and was acquired by Mr. Roberts in August of 2003. One of the City's most famous boutique hotels, the Roberts Mayfair sits in the center of the convention district. This 18 story 182-room hotel consists primarily of luxury suites.

Roberts Tower is one of the Roberts's most exciting and aggressive projects.

A 24 story all-glass tower adjacent to the existing Roberts Mayfair Hotel that will include 58 for sale luxury condos, a new four star restaurant, a spa and exercise room, and new meeting rooms for the Mayfair Hotel. Roberts Tower on the Plaza is designed to achieve LEED Gold certification for environmentally sustainable and responsible construction.

Roberts Crowne Plaza Hotel, Marietta –Atlanta

1775 Parkway Place, NW Marietta GA 3067 770-428-4400
The Roberts Mayfair Hotel -Atlanta is conveniently located off Interstate 75, just 15 minutes from downtown Atlanta and 25 minutes from Hartsfield Airport.

Roberts Comfort Inn-Busch Gardens,
Tampa

820 Busch Blvd
Tampa, FL 33612

813-933-4011
The 257 room hotel includes a large conference center.

Roberts Holiday Inn – Houston, SW

11160 SW Freeway
Houston, TX 77031
281-530-1400

The Roberts Holiday
Inn, Houston SW is a
207 room hotel with
conference and banquet facilities.

Roberts Radisson Hotel– Spartanburg, SC

9027 Fairforest Rd
Spartanburg, SC
29301 864-574-2111

The Roberts
Radisson Hotel in
Spartanburg, SC is a
200 room hotel with conference
facilities.

Roberts Holiday Inn – Shreveport, LA

1419 E 70th St
Shreveport, LA 71105
318-797-9900

The Roberts Holiday Inn
in Shreveport, LA is 267
room hotel.

Roberts Orpheum Theater – a historic and unique entertainment venue adjacent to the Roberts Mayfair Hotel.

The Roberts Orpheum Theater opened in 1917 as the Orpheum vaudeville theatre, decorated in lavishly ornamented beaux-arts style; it remained in the original owner's family until purchased

by Michael and Steven Roberts in 2004. With seating capacity of 1,500, the Roberts Orpheum Theater will offer midsize touring theatrical shows and local productions

concerts and non-ticketed corporate, weddings and special events.

Roberts Aviation owns two aircraft, a Gulfstream III, 12-passenger luxury business jet; and, a Hawker 8 passenger, mid size jet. Million Air in Dallas, TX manages operations.

Roberts Isle and Resort – the largest
African -American owned development in the
Bahamas.

Roberts Isle and Resort is a 50 -
unit condominium and luxury
gated community with boat
docks, swimming pool and
tennis courts, in Sandy Port,
near Nassau.

Mr. Roberts has served on the Board of Directors of the
following publicly held companies:
- Alamosa PCS Holdings, Inc. [OTC: ALMO]
- ACME Communications [NASDAQ: ACME]
- USA Network/HSN[NASDAQ: USAI]

He currently serves on the Board of Directors of the
following Organizations:
- International Council of Shopping Centers
- Chairman, National Association of Black Hotel
  Owners, Operators Developers
- National Association of Black Owned Broadcasters

He has been the subject of feature stories in the following
publications:
- Black Enterprise Magazine
- Forbes Magazine
- Success Magazine
- St. Louis Commerce Magazine (Cover Story)
- Business Week
- Kappa Alpha Psi Journal (Cover Story)
- The Black Collegian Magazine
- US Department of Transporation,"Transportation Link"
- St. Louis Business Journal

A nationally renowned speaker, Mr. Roberts has served as a guest speaker for the following:

- Harvard Business School Conference on Cooperative Economics
- University of Missouri, Columbia School of Business
- Morehouse College Executive Lecture Series
- Northern Ohio Minority Business Council
- Kansas African-American Museum
- Pittsburgh Minority Purchasing Council
- Jackson State University
- St. Louis University School of Business
- Dallas Black Contractors Association
- University of Missouri, St. Louis VISION Speaker Series
- Texas Southern University

Mr. Roberts is a recipient of hundreds of awards including the 2007 Ernst & Young Entrepreneur of the Year Award in Emerging Markets; and, 2008 inductee into the Morehouse College MLK Renaissance Leaders Hall of Fame.

Mr. Roberts is the author of ***Action Has No Season, Secrets and Strategies to Gaining Wealth and Authority***. Book reviews have characterized his work as, "a must read for leaders and entrepreneurs"; "his book proves that Mike Roberts is a capitalist for his time...part existentialist, part-capitalist, he is building a legacy for his family and all aspiring African-Americans who want to participate in the American Dream."

ACTION HAS NO SEASON can be ordered from Mr. Roberts' website as well as Amazon, Barnes & Noble and other major book retailers.

Mr.Roberts received his Juris doctorate degree from St. Louis University in 1974. Prior to graduation from law school, he was selected as a participant in special studies programs at the International Institute of Human Rights, Strasbourg, France (1973); and The Hague Academy of International Law, The Hague, Holland (1972).

The Roberts Companies

1408 No. Kingshighway Suite 300, St. Louis MO 63113 Ph: 314-367-4600 Fax: 314-367-0174 Website: www.michaelvroberts.com

Feature stories
A Legacy of Honoring Entrepreneurial Excellence

For more than two decades Ernst & Young and the Entrepreneur Of The Year awards have honored and celebrated entrepreneurial men and women and the companies they create and grow into market-leading organizations. During that time we have chronicled their capacity to transform organizations, create new products and industries, enrich individual lives, and contribute to the vibrancy of local and national economies.

Entrepreneur Of the Year winners represent companies that are market leaders or have the unmistakable potential to become one. They are among the most influential and recognizable names and brands in the world—Jeff Bezos of Amazon, com, Steve Case of America Online, Wayne Huizenga of Blockbuster, Pierre Omidyar of eBay, Howard Schultz of Starbucks Corp., and Kevin Plank of Under Armour.

The annual Entrepreneur Of The Year awards begin each year with programs across the United States. Seven to 10 winners in varying award categories in each program are selected from among nominees by independent panels of judges, comprising local business, financial, academic and media figures. In 2007, 26 U.S. regions hosted Entrepreneur Of The Year awards and honored their winners at awards banquets during the month of June. All regional winners become contenders for the national awards.

National Entrepreneur Of The Year winners are chosen in one of 10 national categories by independent judging panels under the auspices of the Ewing Marion Kauffman Foundation. From those winners, judges narrow their selection to one person—an individual whose leadership and overall entrepreneurial excellence clearly sets him or her apart. That person is honored as the Ernst & Young Entrepreneur Of The Year and represents the United States at the World Entrepreneur Of The Year event, which takes place in Monte Carlo. See page 42 for more about World Entrepreneur Of The Year and the 2007 winner.

Entrepreneur Of The Year judges have firsthand knowledge of what it takes to grow and lead a successful business. Many are past national or regional Entrepreneur Of The Year winners themselves. They have experienced the rewards and challenges of building winning enterprises and understand that success is not measured in dollars alone. Judges take a number of factors into consideration when making their decisions, including the type of business, its everyday practices with respect to employees, and its impact on the community.

National Ernst & Young Entrepreneur Of The Year winners and finalists are announced at an annual awards gala, the culmination of the Entrepreneur Of The Year event held in November at the Desert Springs JW Marriott Resort & Spa in Palm Springs. As part of the event, all regional and national winners are also inducted into the elite Entrepreneur Of The Year Hall of Fame, on permanent display at Ernst & Young's U.S. headquarters building at 5 Times Square in New York City.

The following pages will introduce you to the 2007 judges and our Ernst & Young Entrepreneur Of The Year winners and finalists. Find out what makes them stand out as examples of entrepreneurial excellence.

For complete information on the Entrepreneur Of The Year awards program visit www.ey.com/us/eoy or call 1-800-755-AWARD.

rothers and business partners Michael and Steven Roberts founded Roberts Hotels Group (RHG) m 2003 with the purchase of their first property, the historic Mayfair Hotel in downtown St. Louis. Combined with their latest forays into the hospitality industry, the Roberts' ongoing real estate ventures have helped to stimulate the revitalization of often depressed and predominantly African-American sections of cities across the country.

The Mayfair, a St. Louis fixture since 1917, was in disrepair at the time of its acquisition, but the brothers had a desire to contribute to the revitalization of their hometown. According to president and COO Steve Roberts, refurbishing the Mayfair was just the first step. "It created additional real estate opportunities, because we asked ourselves what we could do to make that piece of property more successful." The Mayfair became the hub for subsequent development, including a 24-story condominium project innovatively connected so that residents can avail themselves of the hotel's amenities, including exercise, concierge and dining services.

EMERGING
Michael V Roberts (left)
Chairman, CEO, Founder
Steven C. RobertsPresident, COO, Founder
Roberts Hotels Group St. Louis, Mo.
Founded: 2003

St. Louis is also the site of one of RHG's most recent acquisitions earlier this year, which will be unveiled soon as the Roberts Ultra Hotel and Spa, "the model for our ventures going forward," according to Michael Roberts, chairman and CEO. "We're real estate guys," he says, "and buying existing buildings that are undervalued is the model that makes sense to us. We can then turn it around into a reasonably priced, good-quality hotel for Americans who are now more mobile and looking for better vacation opportunities or places to conduct business."

Today, RHG owns and manages 11 hotels, primarily in the Midwest and South, increasing the company's employment base from 50 to well over 1,000 workers. The development provides local jobs and infuses new life into distressed urban areas. "We look at it not only as a business, but as a commitment to a community and an industry," Steve explains. "You can't have arm's-length commitment. You have to roll up your sleeves and get your hands dirty. The people in a new venture must learn to understand that your commitment is as great as, or greater than, their own."

"Entrepreneurial" is an apt description of the Roberts brothers' careers. "An entrepreneur is a visionary, someone who looks beyond what's there today, and is something of a risk-taker," says Steve. Roberts Hotels Group is just the latest in more than 70 ventures over the last three decades—beginning with Roberts-Roberts & Associates, a consulting and construction management firm, as well as highly successful broadcasting and wireless businesses.

"We look at it not only as a business, but as a commitment to community and an industry".

"Entrepreneurial" is an apt description of the Roberts brothers' careers. "An entrepreneur is a visionary, someone who looks beyond what's there today, and is something of a risk-taker," says Steve. Roberts Hotels Group is just the latest in more than 70 ventures over the last three decades—beginning with Roberts-Roberts & Associates, a consulting and construction management firm, as well as highly successful broadcasting and wireless businesses.

And success is what Michael and Steven expect of each of their companies. "We're proud of our achievement in growing the hotel division so quickly," says Steve, "but this business is a stand-alone company with independent management" that must earn a profit, and does.

Following RHG's development of the Mayfair in St. Louis, the brothers evolved a pattern of taking over existing hotels and investing in the staff their brand of personal management care. RHG properties in Atlanta, Dallas, Tampa, Houston, Spartanburg (S.C), Shreveport (La.), and Ft. Myers (Fla.) were name-brand hotels before becoming part of the Roberts Hotels Group. That strategy of working with larger, more established hotel brands has helped to propel RHG into the hospitality mainstream in only five years. "We like the hotel management side," says Steve, "and we don't think anyone manages as well as we do, from an owner's perspective."

That management acumen includes effectively balancing risk

Steven and Michael Roberts (Right) accept the prestigious Ernst & Young Entrepreneur of the Year Award, 2007

"Fake It Till You Make It"

Tomas Kellner, 10.16.00

EVERY ENTREPRENEUR KNOWS how to bluff. Michael Roberts and his brother Steven have refined the practice into high art. A couple of years ago the small-time businessmen from North St. Louis decided to cash in on the wireless craze. With no experience in the trade, they approached Thomas Mateer, vice president of affiliations at Sprint PCS in Kansas City, and put an offer on the table. Instead of Sprint's having to deal with dozens of little telcos in rural Missouri, the Robertses would build the cell phone network themselves and take a 90% piece of the action. They'd pay for the entire project themselves—$74 million in total, including $34 million for transmission equipment, $7 million for retail outlets and $13 million for the licenses and equipment in two small urban markets Sprint owned. The pitch was dubious. The brothers had dabbled in soul food, in consulting and in real estate in the worst part of St. Louis, as well as in a couple of little-watched home shopping UHF TV stations. Still, they were convincing, since they ended up with a deal. "Of course, I told Sprint I had the money for what I needed to do", says Mike, 51. Just one problem: He really didn't have that kind of dough—or any easy way of getting it. Mike approached Nortel Networks, which was providing equipment for the Sprint franchise, and hit it up for a loan. Nortel agreed to match the $18 million in equity that they had from past deals. Hardly enough. So Mike took his offer to a competitor. "I told Lucent, how would you like to have Missouri, and take it from Nortel? "he recalls. Lucent agreed to a

$56 million loan to Roberts Wireless Communications, with an interest rate of 4.5% above Libor, and took the company as collateral. "We grab at a chance and then figure out how we're going to do it and how we're going to pay for it," Mike laughs." Fake it till you make it." And make it they did. In ten months they built a wireless system with 12,000 clients in an area with 1.5 million potential customers. But instead of staying in the business they flipped it to Alamosa Holdings, a Sprint affiliate, for $400 million in cash and stock, which included $56 million in assumed debt. This sort of chicanery can't be learned overnight. The brothers grew up in a middle-class family of six, in a segregated area of St. Louis. Their mother was a teacher; their father, who now serves as their chief financial officer, worked for the post office. The kids had big ambitions. Both put themselves through college and law school with scholarships, and briefly entered local politics in the late 1970s."I learned to come across as if I were succeeding," Mike says. "No one really wants to be in the presence of someone who is broke or looks broke." His life in business— and acting—started after he graduated from St. Louis University's law school. Mike passed himself off as a consultant and began advising corporations on how to avoid discrimination and sexual harassment suits. "My lawyer friend put me in a Lincoln Continental and let me wear his seersucker suits to meetings," he says. With the little bit in fees that came in, Roberts invested in run-down urban real estate that he bought for next to nothing, remodeled and sold for a profit. Steve, now 48, joined Mike in 1977, and together they bought an abandoned 200,000-square-foot building from Sears, Roebuck for $20,000 in cash, and a $500,000 loan from the retailer and a bank. Totally refurbished, the urban mall has 50 minority-run businesses and services, from clothes shops to Chinese take-out and a high school equivalency testing center. The brothers still keep their offices there—a telling study in contrasts: Mike's is dark, cavernous, filled with African art and heavy wooden chairs shaped like elephants; Steve's is light, functional and sparsely decorated. They've since bought and are developing several shopping centers and office buildings. Real estate is nice, but the Robertses wanted a different kind of action, too. Each had served as an alderman on the St. Louis city council, and they'd sat in on many cable television hearings, a quick course in broadcasting. When they applied for and got a UHF TV license in 1985, they didn't have the money to build the station. Mike convinced Home Shopping Network to put up a $3.8 million loan, in addition to $1.6 million a year for carrying the show on the channel. Suddenly he had a station. These days a computer runs the channel. A single operator feeds ad tapes and controls Home Shopping programming via satellite link—at close to zero labor cost. The brothers replicated that model in Denver and spent the 1990s building TV stations in Raleigh-Durham, Albuquerque, Salt Lake City and Hartford. Then they sold off all but the Denver operation to Acme Communications and Paxson Communications, for $21 million in cash and stock. Today their enterprises, collectively called Roberts Cos., gross $30 million a year; 90% of their 200 employees are blacks and Hispanics. The Robertses are worth at least $300 million (given the drop in Alamosa's stock), although they claim that estimate is way too low. No resting on laurels here. In May Mike bought a $5 million Hawker jet, with the idea of starting a charter company. He wants to privatize telecoms in the Caribbean. "In the business world there's a barrel of small fish and a fast stream with the big fish," he says." I could sit here and cut grass or repair cars and call myself a business. But I'm trying to catch the whale. I'm looking for Moby-Dick."

Roberts brothers oversee growing $460 million, 34-company empire.

BY PAM DROOG

On a recent Sunday in Atlanta, a few guys got together for brunch before the National Basketball Association All-Star game. The group included former President Bill Clinton; former Atlanta mayor Maynard Jackson; former Atlanta mayor and United States ambassador to the United Nations Andrew Young; Perry Christie, the prime minister of the Bahamas; and St. Louis businessmen and former Aldermen Mike and Steve Roberts. "The one person who knew everyone was me," says Mike Roberts.

When they're not dining with dignitaries, the Roberts brothers might be making phone calls, attending meetings or considering deals on behalf of The Roberts Companies, a diversified $460 million, 34-company empire. Holdings range from real estate development to business consulting, television stations to wireless communications, aviation to construction...even a gated community in the Bahamas. Mike is chairman of the board and Steve is president of the company. Each division is named Roberts—even Roberts Isle. And why not— they've earned it. "We've been breaking down barriers as long as we can remember," says Steve Roberts.

THE VILLAGE

The hub of all things Roberts is the Victor Roberts Building, a former Sears store on North Kingshighway at Martin Luther King Blvd. The brothers bought it in 1982 and named it for their father who retired from the U.S. Postal Service after 39 years; he's chief financial officer of The Roberts Companies. Today his namesake building houses an eclectic mix of 50-plus restaurants, retail shops and service businesses. On the top floor are the Roberts' corporate offices and the master control studio for their television stations. The brothers were born just a couple of blocks away and spent their early years nearby. They have a younger brother, Mark, who now works in the Denver office and will manage the company's upcoming Jackson, Miss. office later this year. The youngest Roberts, Lori, works in the company's St. Louis office.

From a young age, the two brothers were devoted to each other, and to excellence. "We were always linked together," says Mike, who's three-and-a-half years older than Steve. "We were pretty much interested in achieving our goals, and in working."

The brothers cut grass, shoveled snow, delivered newspapers. "In college I had a little business trying to sell dashikis (colorful shirts) and African paraphernalia to bookstores," Mike says.

Both Roberts attended college as Danforth fellows. Mike attended Lindenwood University, then earned a J.D. degree from Saint Louis University School of Law in 1974. He also attended the Hague Academy of International Law in the Netherlands. Mike had considered a career in medicine, since the most successful African Americans he saw were doctors. "I also thought of being an Episcopal priest, because in that role I could pontificate to people on Sunday mornings," Mike says. "But I realized if I went to law school and got into politics I could pontificate every day."

Steve attended Clark University in Massachusetts. Like Mike, he considered careers in medicine and ministry, "but I think we both realized independently our destinies were in different directions," he says. He also returned to St. Louis for law school, earning a J.D. and L.L.M. at Washington University.

While Steve studied law, Mike launched Roberts-Roberts & Associates, in 1974. "We never planned to practice law," Mike explains. He believes "law school is a great extended liberal arts education that also teaches you a new language, how to think, how to perceive opportunities more quickly."

Mike perceived an opportunity based on his knowledge of Title VII law and how it addressed discrimination in the workplace. "At the time a lot of big companies had big class-action lawsuits against them that cost hundreds of millions of dollars," he says. "So we had their attention." Roberts-Roberts & Associates worked with public and private sector clients including Nooter Corporation, Anheuser-Busch, Southwestern Bell, Bi-State Development, MoDOT and others, consulting on increasing participation of minority and women-owned businesses in multi-million-dollar capital construction projects.

At the same time, Mike pursued his goal of seeking elective office. He'd always been active in college and community politics, but he got a real taste of the lifestyle in 1976, when he was Jimmy Carter's campaign manager in St. Louis. "When he was elected I was at the White House every month," Mike says. He played tennis with Hamilton Jordan, Carter's chief of staff, and hob-nobbed with cabinet members. "It was quite an illuminating experience," he recalls. The following year, 1977, at age 28, he became the youngest person ever elected to the St. Louis Board of Aldermen—that is, until Steve, age 26, was elected two years later.

ON THE BOARD

"Being an alderman is one of the best experiences you can have," Steve says. "I was in a good position to do a lot of good." He was the chief sponsor of the St. Louis Centre and Union Station developments, and Mike was the force behind Grand Center. They both had a hand in Laclede's Landing and Gateway Mall redevelopment.

Longtime friend Mike Jones, executive director of the Greater St. Louis Regional Empowerment Zone, served with the Roberts on the Board of Aldermen. "It was me, Mike, Steve, Virvus Jones and Wayman Smith, the political equivalent of the Temptations. We had a great time every Friday and put on a great show!" Jones recalls. "Each of us five guys were strong individual leaders, but we always found a way to support each other even when we occasionally disagreed." Though he has been in public service a long time, Jones says, "that period will always stand out as the highlight of my public life."

(left to right): **MIKE JONES, STEVE ROBERTS, MIKE ROBERTS, WAYMAN SMITH** and **VIRVUS JONES** -served together as Aldermen in the early 80's

Despite their accomplishments, Mike left the board in 1983 and Steve in 1991. "We both feel that government service needs to be rotated. New ideas should come in," Mike says. "But just because you're not elected, that doesn't mean you can't serve. We believed now we needed to put our money where our mouth used to be."

As a result, in the past two decades, Mike and Steve have invested about $25 million in commercial and residential redevelopment in the city through Roberts Brothers Development. "In this environment we have our own laboratory, creating jobs and making sure folks can take care of their families," Mike says. "We had political empowerment, but now we have economic empowerment, which is much more real and tangible."

At one point the brothers owned about 90 residential units. Other acquisitions include the Victor Roberts Building; a 40,000-square-foot strip mall at Kingshighway and Delmar plus surrounding properties; the former W.K. Woods Stationery building at 209 N. 4th St.; the former St. Louis School Board headquarters at 911 Locust St.; Roberts Village a 27,000-square-foot development at Martin Luther King and Kingshighway; and a 42,000-square-foot center being built behind the Victor Roberts Building, earned Mike and Steve the Mayor's Spirit of St. Louis Award last year.

"Every banker I talked to said that's not a good location. So we set an example and put up a $4 million strip mall ourselves," Mike says. "Now those bankers are saying please let us refinance you!"

TV STATIONS AND TOWERS

One day in 1981, the Roberts met a man who knew another man who wanted to meet African Americans who might be interested in owning a TV station. "We said, why not? We both had backgrounds in communications," Steve says. At the time, minorities had an advantage when applying for a broadcast license. The Roberts did their homework and applied. "The challenge was, everyone else applying for the license also was an African American so we were back to a level playing field," Steve says. "But that was the genesis of Roberts Broadcasting."

Another challenge was it took six years to actually get the license. And when they got it, they had no programming for it. "We talked to religious broadcasters, shopping networks, everybody," Steve says. "We met the founders of Home Shopping Network and established a strategic partnership with them. We'd take their programming off the satellite and they'd pay us to broadcast it in this market."

The new station owners still were missing one vital component: a broadcasting facility. "The original TV stations in the market were built in the 1940s and '50s, so building a new one was a major undertaking," Steve says. The station, WRBU-TV Channel 46, which became a UPN affiliate in April, was the first new full-power television station in the St. Louis market in 20 years, and it's the first fully automated station in the U.S.

Armed with the experience of establishing one TV station, the Roberts built 11 more and sold eight of them to various broadcasting companies. Today the company owns and operates TV stations in St. Louis and Denver. The brothers hope to build stations in Columbia, S.C. and Jackson, Miss.

HOLD THE PHONE

Building all those TV towers, the Roberts gained expertise in construction, which led to the establishment of Roberts Construction Company in 1989. An affiliated business, Roberts

Tower Company, locates, designs, builds and owns towers for television stations—and for the wireless communication industry.

"When we went through the painful process of putting together our first TV station, we also learned how the system works and became familiar with emerging technologies," Steve says. "That led to our bidding at the FCC auctions for wireless-phone licenses, and that led to Roberts Wireless." Again, the Roberts got their licenses—but needed the equipment and hardware to use them. That would cost about $65 million. Their clever solution was to make a deal with Sprint PCS to become an affiliate and return the government licenses. With the help of Lucent Technologies, which loaned them $56 million for equipment and construction, Roberts Wireless developed Sprint's PCS network in all of Missouri except St. Louis and KC, plus parts of Illinois, Kansas, Oklahoma and Arkansas. It was the only PCS company wholly-owned by African Americans in the nation. The company's first Sprint PCS store opened Feb. 2, 1999 in Jefferson City. The late Governor Mel Carnahan and Lt. Gov. Roger Wilson attended the ribbon cutting.

But the brothers didn't stop there. In summer 2000, Roberts Wireless merged with Alamosa PCS Holdings Inc., another Sprint PCS affiliate, for $4 million cash and 13.5 million shares of stock, about $280 million at the time. Alamosa also took over the $56 million loan from Lucent. The brothers kept their 154 Sprint PCS towers.

All this activity caught the attention of Forbes, Success and Black Enterprise magazine, which listed the Roberts' broadcasting and wireless communications companies among the largest minority owned businesses in the United States.

IF IT FITS...

"We are diversified," Mike says. "I always felt that's important. If you limit yourself to one sector of business opportunities in this economy, you die." But, he explains, there is a logical connection between, for example, a wireless phone company and downtown office buildings. "A large part of building a wireless phone company is buying the real estate for the towers," Mike says.

A real estate deal also was the catalyst for Roberts Steak & Buffet restaurant. The brothers bought a restaurant property complete with equipment and a good I-270 location. "We thought let's reopen it, and we found someone to run it," Steve says. The restaurant was sold to Cracker Barrel in May.

The aviation division, Roberts Aviation, was founded in 2000. "That fit with our other companies, because we had made a big sale and needed an appropriate tax shelter," Mike says. The company owns and leases a 12-passenger luxury Gulfstream III and a mid-size eight passenger Hawker. "They earn their keep," he adds.

Then there's Roberts Isle, the brothers' Bahamas property located near Nassau. "That put us into international business," Mike says. The Roberts, who have private homes in the area and have been visiting there for more than 25 years, are working on permits for a $25 million, 54-unit residential development on 2.5 acres.

"We probably have someone submitting some kind of deal to us almost daily," Steve says. "If it makes that first cut, or if we have a business related to it, we'll look at the numbers, put a plan together and run it past our experts. None of them is ever shocked or tells us, this time you've gone too far."

Adds Kay Gabbert, senior vice president of the Roberts Companies, "Our philosophy typically is, if there's an opportunity, let's go for it. We never say no. We always want next year to be different from this year, and it has been that way for the three of us for 21 years."

INVOLVED AND COMMITTED

It's hard to pick up a local publication and not find one or both Roberts brothers mentioned, not just for their business activities, but also for their leadership roles in professional and civic organizations. Mike is or has been a board member of the St. Louis Community College Foundation, United Way, Better Family Life, Home Shopping Network, Acme Communications and Alamosa PCS. Steve also serves on the Alamosa PCS board, as well as Allegiant Bank, Falcon Products and Silver King Communications. He's vice chairman of the board of MERS/Goodwill, and also a board member of the Muny, the Repertory Theatre, the Missouri Historical Society, the Fair St. Louis Foundation, St. Patrick's Center, the AIDS Foundation, St. Louis Black Leadership Roundtable and Whitfield School.

In addition, Steve is vice chairman of the Regional Business Council and a member of the RCGA's Leadership Circle. From that perspective, he says he'd like to see more business people get involved in their communities. "I'd like to see them take just five percent of their time and become mentors, work with Red Cross, serve on local theatre boards, visit seniors or tutor children," he says. Mike adds, "It's not a sin to make a lot of money. It's a sin when you don't know how to reinvest through contributions back into the community to make a better society in which you operate your business."

More of Mike's business philosophies soon will be available in a book he's writing, Action Has No Season: Understanding the

Complexities of Gaining Wealth and Authority. "Basically it's for my kids," he says. "It's the things you don't learn in school." Mike and his wife Jeanne have four children, including a twin son and daughter who will graduate next year from Pepperdine University School of Law—and join The Roberts Companies. Steve and his wife Eva Frazer, M.D., have three children.

In their free time, the brothers like to work. "We work seven days a week, not in the office, but we're always thinking about the business," Steve says. Adds Mike, "If you enjoy what you're doing you never work a day in your life."

Actually, they like to play tennis and ski. "We have always liked to fish," Mike says. "Now, we do it at our own place in the Bahamas!"

Have things turned out the way they expected? "No, because we never expected anything," Steve says. "Did we expect we'd be in the wireless communications business, or the tower business, or own a TV station? No! When we were growing up, those things would have been in our furthest fantasies, as alien as building condos on the moon."

Roberts Earthview Village...now there's an opportunity.

Pam Droog is a frequent contributor to St. Louis Commerce Magazine.

The Kings of Kingshighway

The Roberts brothers fight to bring back life to north St. Louis

BY SHELLEY SMITHSON

shelly.smithson@riverfronttimes.com

Mike and Steve Roberts sipped their apple martinis and savored the moment. One thousand guests had gathered in the Starlight Room of the Chase Park Plaza Hotel to celebrate the launch of UPN affiliate WRBU-TV (Channel 46), the Robertses' latest television venture. Steve Roberts, the younger and more soft-spoken of the two brothers, grabbed a microphone and quieted the crowd. "Shhh!" he teased. "I know the drinks are good!"

"Many of you know that Mike and I served in public office," he began on that cool April evening last year. "We served on the board of aldermen and, for many years, we had the opportunity to work as colleagues with our good friend

[Mayor] Francis Slay. And we want to ask Francis to come up here."

The Fabulous Motown Revue piped up their horns as the mayor took the stage and proclaimed it UPN 46 Day. The mayor passed the microphone to a parade of UPN stars, including Jerry Springer, the king of talk-show trash. Springer thanked the Roberts brothers for picking up his show and joked, "It doesn't say much about their taste. Frankly, it's great to be here in St.

Louis. This is where we get most of our guests!"

The crowd giggled and groaned and returned to their cosmopolitans. Mike Roberts sauntered from room to room, walking across the floor illuminated by the UPN logo, past the wine bar and the ice sculpture of the Arch and outside to the rooftop balcony of the Chase. From here, Mike could look down on his stately white-stone home near the corner of Lindell Boulevard and Kingshighway and his brother's manse one street north on Westmoreland Place. To the east he could see downtown, where he and Steve have become major players in the redevelopment of the Old Post Office District.

The air was crisp and the sky was clear, a perfect evening for guests to peer through the telescope perched atop the hotel's roof, pointed at the UPN headquarters in the old Sears building on North Kingshighway between Page and Martin Luther King boulevards. The brothers bought the vacant department store in 1982 and christened it the Victor Roberts Building in honor of their father, a retired U.S. postal worker.

From this spot in one of St. Louis' most downtrodden neighborhoods — two blocks from their childhood home – the Robertses have risen from black middle-class roots to amass a multimillion-dollar empire of 35 companies, including TV stations, television and cell-phone towers, consulting businesses and real estate holdings in the United States and the Bahamas.

The Victor Roberts Building, with its 50-plus shops and government offices, has brought some stability to the neighborhood. But still the area remains the long-forgotten stepsister of the Central West End, the thriving neighborhood less than a mile south. The Roberts brothers are bent on changing that. Working with the city, they have unfurled an ambitious blueprint they believe will begin to transform the pockmarked face of north St. Louis. The Robertses hope that, in the process, they will see the collapse of the Berlin Wall of racial segregation that has haunted this city for generations.

The plan is to extend the Central West End northward with homes, condos and retail outlets, infusing life into a huge swath of urban decay between Washington Boulevard to the south, Taylor Avenue to the east, Martin Luther King Drive to the north, and Union Boulevard to the west.

Although best known for their downtown development plans, including a $17 million renovation of the Mayfair Hotel, restoring a semblance of vitality to moribund north St. Louis is what really stirs the brothers' passion.

"Our vision is to have a very diverse neighborhood," Steve Roberts explains. "It shouldn't be one racial or economic group, [and] we'd like to see empty-nesters come back to where their parents or grandparents may have lived. This is our home. That's what motivates us."

Of course, there are other reasons too for this high-energy development duo (Mike is 55 years old; Steve is 51) who, in the 1970s began to tap into the white power structure by advising worried chief executives on how to avoid the specter of major class-action lawsuits by increasing minority employment. After all, they don't call themselves "straightup, hard-core capitalists" for nothing.

"The housing stock is good [and] the land is priced so far under the market," says Mike Roberts. "People who are not seeing the opportunity here are going to be shaking their heads in a few years."

As kids the Roberts brothers witnessed the sting of racial

hostility. They grew up watching blocks busted, public swimming pools segregated and blacks relegated to only the right-field seats at Sportsman's Park. They realize racial tensions linger still and are keenly aware of the obstacles ahead. Few investors, developers and bankers are willing to cross Delmar, a demarcation line in St. Louis' racially and economically segregated landscape.

Two years ago the banks refused to loan the Robertses $4 million to build a 42,000-square-foot shopping center on Page behind the Victor Roberts Building. "They said, 'We're not certain about this neighborhood,'" Mike Roberts recalls. The brothers chose to build the strip mall with their own money and opened it last year. But how, they ask, can small business owners in the area ever finance even the smallest loans to remodel their buildings and resurrect their community if banks are unwilling to take a chance on north St. Louis?

At the age of 26, Mike Roberts (left) was the city's youngest alderman --until his brother, Steve, was sworn into office at age 25.

"The question is: Can the private sector, banks and private developers, local residents and the city work to bring an

entire neighborhood back together comprehensively — not just tearing down a building here and there?" Steve Roberts asks. "We have to expand the horizon. If we don't do this, if we don't encourage

people to open their perspectives, then frankly, it may never get done."

The north St. Louis boyhood home of Mike and Steve Roberts still stands at 4641 Vernon Avenue, a red-brick two-story flat with burglar bars on its front door. Trash collects on the vacant lot across the street from the rental home and junk cars fill a neighbor's backyard.

From the beginning, the brothers were close, devoted to and protective of each other. Steve remembers sitting on a rocking horse inside their living room when he was three years old. Six-year-old Mike sensed something was wrong and pushed his little brother off and out of harm's way, just as the heavy plaster ceiling caved in.

"I've been saving him ever since," Mike jokes.

When Steve smiles, which he does often, laugh lines form around his brown eyes and his face looks young, even though his hairline is retreating. His complexion is cinnamon, his build slim. He and Mike both stand six-foot-one, but Mike has broad shoulders, lighter skin, emerald-green eyes and a graceful white streak that parts his black hair on the right.

"When you look at pictures of the kids in my grandmother's side of the family, they are every size, shape and color of the spectrum," Steve says, explaining that his mother's ancestors were African, American Indian and white.

Just three months ago, on a business trip to Mississippi, the Roberts brothers learned that their father's grandfather was Wright Roberts, the son of an African woman and a white plantation owner. It seems that Wright inherited land from his white father and established a prominent family farm near West Point, Mississippi. He also was able to send his son, Squire Victor Roberts, to medical school. That son later moved to St. Louis during the 1920s, where he worked as a physician in the African-American neighborhood near Market and Jefferson.

In 1922 Dr. Roberts' son, Victor, was born in the Ville, a thriving African-American neighborhood northeast of Martin Luther King and Taylor. "We had doctors, lawyers, grocery stores, cleaners, taxi cabs," remembers 81-year-old Victor Roberts. "We couldn't go to Grand Avenue, to the movies or restaurants, but we had all that in our neighborhood — bowling, dance halls, the YMCA. Everybody worked together and lived next to each other — janitors and teachers and doctors."

After his father died, Victor went to work for the U.S. Postal Service before joining the 92nd Infantry Division, one of only two African- American infantry units in World War II. When he returned from Europe, he married Delores Talley, whose family had migrated to St. Louis from the Missouri boot heel.

"We were pretty much sheltered as a middle-class African-American family," Mike explains. "We were taught
traditional work habits and values. We were altar boys in the Episcopal Church."

Delores made sure her children were exposed to the arts and cultural activities. Steve remembers being dragged out of bed on Saturday mornings to take science classes at Oak Knoll Park in Clayton and trying out for a play in the dead of winter at the American Theatre. "We were never bored," Mike says, "because Mom would always have some interesting project for us to do."

The Roberts family lived with Victor's mother in the two-family home on Vernon until their third son, Mark, was born in 1958. They then moved to a new, segregated neighborhood of fourteen ranch-style houses that had just been built northeast of Natural Bridge Road and North Kingshighway. Everyone who lived in the houses surrounding the new subdivision was white.

"That's the first time I knew I was even black," Steve recalls. "One time I was playing baseball with these kids who were white. We were in my backyard and there was this big redneck-looking guy who came out of this four-family flat behind our home.

"He comes out and grabs his son and says, 'You can't play with him because he's a nigger.' I didn't even know what a nigger was at six years old."

Steve went inside and asked his mom. "She told me how when she was a kid, she and her friends would go to the Fox Theatre with her sister, who was darker, and she couldn't get in. But my mom was fair-complected, so she would beat the system by sneaking in without them knowing. This was the first time I realized that there was a discrepancy in the way citizens of this country were treated."

As more middle-class black families moved to the tidy new neighborhood, whites began moving out. "They block-busted the place," Mike explains. "The realtors courted white people, saying, 'You have black people in the neighborhood, your prices are going to go down.'

"And as a result, they ran at cheap prices and these Realtors would pick up the properties and turn around and sell them to black families for a lot more than they paid for them."

Victor and Delores Robertsstillllivein thenorthSt.Louis ranch home they moved into in 1958. Thebrotherscredit theirsuccessto their parents.

Like Victor and Delores Roberts, many middle-class black families stayed in the well-to-do neighborhoods of north St. Louis. But over the years, plenty of others moved to the suburbs, just as whites did in the 1960s.

Many feel the black middle-class migration was due largely to a misguided development plan dubbed the Team 4 Report, a city sponsored consultant's study that advocated withholding city services from mostly African-American and low-income neighborhoods. The idea was to make living conditions so bad that black people would eventually move from the city.

On a summer morning in 1976, Mike and Steve Roberts were in New York City attending the Democratic National Convention as delegates from Missouri. Mike, who was Jimmy Carter's campaign manager in St. Louis, had recently become the first African American admitted to the Missouri Athletic Club, the swank downtown haunt of high rolling attorneys. So when the Roberts brothers went to New York, they chose to stay at the nation's oldest and best Athletic Club.

Steve recalls going downstairs to the club's laundry to pick up his and Mike's shirts. The manager told him, "You make sure you go deliver them to these people directly. Don't lollygag or anything." Steve explained to the manager that the shirts were for himself and his brother, who was a member. "I don't believe you," Steve recalls the man saying.

He took the shirts and left. "Of course, we reported it later," he says. "Anytime we would get challenges like that, we'd bring it to the attention of the leadership of the organizations so it wouldn't happen again."

By then Mike was working as a lawyer on antidiscrimination cases with Margaret Bush Wilson, one of the first female African-American attorneys in Missouri and, at the time, the chairwoman of the National Association for the Advancement of Colored People.

Mike graduated from Northwest High School, St. Louis' first desegregated high school, in 1967, then went to Forest Park Community College where he met Virvus Jones. There the two young activists mourned the death of Martin Luther King Jr., marched against the Vietnam War, formed the Black Student Association and fought to bring black-studies programs to colleges. Later, they worked together in HOME (Help Other Men Emerge), a civil-rights organization that preached economic empowerment for black men.

After completing his undergraduate degree at Lindenwood University in St. Charles, Mike graduated from law school at Saint Louis University in 1974 with the help of a grant from the Danforth Foundation and money he earned selling dashikis. Steve attended Clark College in Massachusetts and law school at Washington University as a Danforth scholar.

Fresh out of law school, the brothers launched a consulting firm that over the years has spearheaded increased minority participation in multimillion-dollar capital construction projects for Anheuser-Busch, Dulles and National airports in Washington, D.C., and Lambert St. Louis International Airport.

In 1974 Mike talked his dad into getting a $7,000 loan from the post office credit union to buy a house. He lived in it while he fixed it up, then resold it for a profit and started buying more properties. He also flung himself into politics. In 1977, at the age of 26, Mike became the youngest person ever elected to the city's board of aldermen — that is, until Steve was elected two years later at age 25.

As part of the Black Aldermanic Caucus in the early 1980s, Steve and Mike Roberts, Wayman Smith, Mike Jones and Virvus Jones wrote legislation that required contractors on city-funded projects to hire minority- and women-owned businesses. "Some of the large contractors certainly felt that was radical, that it was un-American, socialist," Steve remembers.

The Robertses also met the city's most powerful developers and learned how to use incentives such as tax-increment financing and tax abatements to lure investors. Steve sponsored redevelopment legislation for Union Station, St. Louis Center and Laclede's Landing. "Had I not been on the board of aldermen, I would have never met these folks," Steve explains. "I didn't run in their social cadre. I didn't attend their country clubs."

It dismayed some members of the black community, however, when Steve in 1994 joined the board of the Veiled Prophet Fair at the urging of the late businessman Bill Maritz. Though the organization was integrated in 1979 and has since changed its name to Fair St. Louis, many blacks remember it for what it was: an all white, all-male society of the super-rich. "Being inside an organization, you can influence change," Steve says of his decision to join.

Mike and Steve concede they've been criticized for "not being black enough." But the notion that light-skinned blacks faced less racism and received greater opportunities is "slave mentality," says Mike. In January 1989, after a decade as an alderman, Mike Roberts decided to challenge incumbent Mayor Vincent Schoemehl Jr. for the party's Democratic nomination. He narrowly lost the race, in part because former U.S. Representative

William Lacy Clay Sr., the era's most powerful African-American politician, supported Schoemehl, who is white. The mayor had agreed to appoint Virvus Jones to the comptroller's job in exchange for Clay's nod.

In 1993, when Steve made his mayoral bid, Clay shunned him as well and threw his support to Freeman Bosley Jr. Steve lost in a landslide to Bosley, who became St. Louis' first black mayor.

"Generally, we didn't get Clay's support because we came up through different channels," Mike explains. "There were certain African-American political heads that had control over wards – Jet Banks and Jordan W. Chambers, which I belonged to. Steve was involved with Leroy Tyus, a very strong political powerhouse. Of course, Clay was one too.

"A lot of these guys, they only wanted someone developed out of their own political backyard," Mike goes on. "That's a narrow-minded approach to creating a level of political empowerment for African Americans."

On the first floor of the Victor Roberts Building, an armed security guard stands at a kiosk. A sign above directs patrons to a beauty supply store, a cell phone outlet, a check-cashing business, a dentist's office and the U.S. Department of Agriculture's Women, Infants and Children program on the second floor.

At a Nation of Islam store, Louis Farrakhan is on television preaching about the "policies of the dragon" in Iraq. Theodore Muhammad says customers stop in to buy newspapers, books and tapes. The smell of fried catfish and hamburgers wafts down the hall from a newly opened grill.

Sue Zambrzuski sits behind a glass display case filled with gold chains and diamond rings at K's Jewelry. She says many of her customers live in the surrounding neighborhoods and walk to this urban mall because they don't have cars. She figures 100 percent of the shoppers are African Americans.

The white people — architects, politicians, contractors and construction workers — who visit immediately head for the Robertses' corporate offices on the third floor, a vastly different world from the mall below.

On a recent morning, Mike Roberts opens the glazed glass double doors and strolls into his cavernous office. An intricately carved oak pool table stands in the middle of the room, surrounded by walls draped with original Native American art and exquisite wood carvings of African warriors and women with their babies.

"We're doing pretty good down here in the 'hood," he quips.

The Roberts brothers' businesses started gaining momentum in the late 1980s when the Federal Communications Commission granted

their first UHF-TV license. Mike convinced the Home Shopping Network to loan them $3.8 million to build a studio on the third floor of the Victor Roberts Building. Since then they've bought and sold stations throughout the southwest and the south. Last year they ditched the Home Shopping Network for UPN, which targets a young, urban audience with a lineup of new and recycled black sitcoms.

But their greatest triumph came in 2001, when the brothers struck gold in the wireless phone market. Mike convinced Sprint that his company could build a PCS network throughout Missouri and the rural Midwest. Needing $95 million to build the network, they put the entire company on the block as collateral and managed to get a loan from Lucent, a network-equipment manufacturer that wanted to break into the Midwest.

The gamble paid off. In six months of nonstop work, the Robertses built the network, then flipped it to a Sprint affiliate for $400 million in cash and stock.

"In politics, you don't have the reward of seeing the final product," Mike explains. "Being in business is like having my own laboratory. I get more out of being able to create real jobs for people."

Mike reclines on a tan leather chair that faces a gas-burning fireplace. On the mantel above — just below the flat-screen TV — sit two replicas of Mike and Steve's private jets, one of which they bought from actor Jim Carrey. They invested in the aircraft as a tax shelter and now rent them to business executives and anyone else who can afford the $3,600 hourly fee.

Mike usually flies out of Lambert rather than using the planes himself. His calendar is booked with speaking engagements around the nation — celebrity events like the NAACP's Image Awards in Los Angeles and real-estate scouting expeditions throughout the United States and the Bahamas with Steve. He and his wife, Jeanne, also frequently visit Malibu, California, where their four children attend Pepperdine University.

In Steve's equally spacious office, about 50 photos of his wife, Dr. Eva Frazer, and their three children (ages ten, fourteen and sixteen) adorn his walls and ultramodern desk. Before choosing to stay home with the kids, Frazer worked as an internist at Barnes-Jewish Hospital. Nowadays she serves on Saint Louis University's board of directors and tag-teams with Steve on chauffeuring their kids to baseball practices, play rehearsals and parties.

When Mike and Steve are both in the office, they usually scarf lunch from the Saint Louis Bread Co. between constant cell phone calls and a packed schedule of appointments. But they never seem hurried. "I get here at nine o' clock and every day is a sprint to keep up," says Jerry Altman, chief counsel for the Roberts Companies.

Jazz music pours out of the office Victor Roberts, the companies' chief financial officer, shares with his daughter, Lori. Mike gives his dad a wave as he strolls down the hall to the conference room, where a team of architects from the Lawrence Group are sitting around an enormous marble table. Everyone jumps up to shake his hand.

The architects are here to brief the brothers on several projects in north St. Louis. "We're playing Monopoly these days," Mike says. They just purchased the vacant Enright School, located northwest of Union and Delmar, from the St. Louis Board of Education for $1 million. They plan to spend $15 million converting the structure, designed by architect William B. Ittner, to upscale apartments and to build at least twenty new houses around it.

"A lot of baby boomers grew up in this neighborhood," Mike says, noting that new homes are being built to the west and that older houses to the south are large and tidy. "Maybe they will be interested in moving back."

Mike and Virvus Jones, now a vice president in the Robertses' real estate firm, kick around the idea of building a nine-hole, par-three golf course at nearby Visitation Park. Mike is wearing black slacks and a bright blue-and-white striped shirt highlighted by cuff links.

His diamond pinkie rink sparkles under the soft lights above.

Steve answers his cell phone as the architects pore over drawings for Roberts Commons. What they envision are 110 residential units and 40,000 square feet of retail space to sprout on the southeast corner of Euclid and Delmar. A condo project — priced from $175,000 to $225,000 — is also in the making on the south side of Washington, just east of Kingshighway.

"Alderman [Terry] Kennedy has written the letter to start a blighting study," Mike tells the men gathered in the room. If the city decides the area around Euclid and Delmar is blighted, the development will be eligible for tax abatement. The Robertses have met with Rodney Crim, executive director of the St. Louis Development Corporation, and Rollin Stanley, the city's Urban Agency Design director, to discuss their plans for the area. Eventually they would like the city to approve a tax-increment financing arrangement to pay for infrastructure improvements and possibly a transportation district, which could finance sidewalk and park upgrades. All of the infrastructure is here — the sewer, the streets, the water, the parks," Steve says. "But it's been completely ignored by the city government." The biggest challenge, however, will be convincing people to cross the "mental demarcation line at Washington," explains Virvus Jones. "The problem is getting people to migrate closer to Delmar. These are mental issues, so you have to do something spectacular." Building a residential and retail complex with parking at the corner of Euclid and Delmar will "complete the block," reasons Jerry Altman, a company vice president. "It will cause people to feel more comfortable."
The Roberts brothers already own a substantial portion of the property along Kingshighway between Delmar and Martin Luther King, including buildings that house Schnucks, Hollywood Video and Blockbuster Video.

Ultimately, the Robertses would like to reopen the Mercedes Club, which they own at 4915 Delmar, and create an even greater impetus for people to move north to the Fountain Park neighborhood, located two blocks from the Central West End.

The Roberts want to revive the stately neighborhood around Fountain Park, just a few blocks north of the Central West End.

At the center of the historic neighborhood are a beautiful, multitiered fountain and an eleven foot bronze statue of Martin Luther King Jr. Most of the huge homes surrounding the park are well-kept, but the surrounding area, like much of north St. Louis, is a hodgepodge of multi- and single-family homes that are either in need of repair or boarded up.

"The Central West End is two minutes from here. But it's twenty years away, from a psychological point of view," Steve says.

Missouri State Senator Patrick Dougherty is standing on a box, pounding his fist on the bar at King Louie's restaurant on Chouteau. "We've got a chance this year to take back the senate!" he shouts. "That's why you're here. That's why you are supporting the Democratic Party!"

Victory cries ring out and Steve Roberts smiles. Even though he and Mike no longer serve in public office, they are still players because of their financial contributions to local, state and national campaigns. This February happy hour, devoted to raising funds for state Democratic senate candidates, is being partially financed by the Robertses.

In 1999 Mike formed the Black PAC, a political action

committee devoted to the "silver rights movement," which he says will create economic opportunities for African Americans. "We found there was a dearth of leadership, particularly in the African-American community, because many who had been there for many years were retiring or passing away, and we needed to encourage bright, committed, honest, credible people to run for office, not just folks who are part of a political organization," Steve explains.

The Robertses and the Black PAC have raised thousands for Mayor Slay, Governor Bob Holden, Senator John Kerry and Al Sharpton, plus scores of candidates for state, local and federal office. Mike was onstage with Kerry as he wowed voters at Forest Park Community College before Missouri's February 3 Democratic primary. He also hosted a fundraiser at his home for Sharpton because he believes the fringe candidate keeps civil-rights and economic-equality issues on the radar.

Not all of the candidates the Roberts brothers support are as popular as Sharpton in the black community. Mayor Slay has been lambasted for his efforts to reform St. Louis public schools by helping to elect a slate of four candidates to take over the school board's majority.

"If you have a school system that is discouraging home ownership, business relocation to the community, or impacting the quality of the future workforce, then what does the mayor of the city do?" Steve counters. "The mayor took a very bold step to say we've got a significant problem here and we've got to address it."

The new board's decision to close sixteen schools (twelve of which were in north St. Louis), to lay off more than 1,000 employees and to outsource scores of other menial jobs to private firms has triggered a tidal wave of resentment in the black community. Now the board is trying to decide whether to close more schools and eliminate gifted programs or force across-the board pay cuts, which would almost certainly lead to a strike by the Local 420 teachers' union.

Jamilah Nasheed, co-chair of the activist group Concerned Citizens Coalition, questions how the Roberts brothers will lure new residents to the city when so much turmoil surrounds the school board's decisions. "When people move into a neighborhood, the first thing they look at is the schools," she says. "If the Robertses want people to move into the neighborhood, they need to make the schools better." The board's actions so far have done the opposite, she claims.

Nasheed lays the blame at the feet of the Black Leadership Roundtable, a group of successful African Americans, including Steve Roberts, who worked with the mayor's office and other business executives to spur the school-board takeover. "The Black Leadership Roundtable are puppets and they move in the interest of the powers that be," she asserts. "In the 1950s and 1960s, individuals of their caliber would have come out to fight this."

Civil-rights activist Percy Green applauds the Roberts brothers for their decision to invest in north St. Louis neighborhoods but cautions that development for middle-and upper-income families should not come at the expense of low-income blacks living in those neighborhoods now.

"We want to see young families of all ethnicities and religions," Steve responds. "We want to see seniors in the area get help preserving their properties."

"We've put our money, our experience, our expertise, our life into this neighborhood," his brother Mike picks up. "We have to be a part of this renaissance of inner-city hard-core areas. If we don't do it, then who will?"

ST. LOUIS POST-DISPATCH

Mike Roberts is a capitalist for his time

By Linda Tucci

He and his brother, Steve, are working to leave a legacy to all of St. Louis, not just African- Americans. The Roberts brothers, Mike and Steve, are moguls. The former city aldermen run a diversified, roughly $500 million company with TV stations, communications towers, charter jets, strip malls, office buildings, downtown lofts, a hotel, a theater and a resort community in the Bahamas. Mike is the visionary. When he graduated law school in 1974 he "just wanted to develop a few neighborhoods." The deals kept coming. By his own admission part-existentialist, part-capitalist, he is building a legacy for his family and all aspiring African-Americans who want to participate in the American Dream. We spoke at company headquarters in north St. Louis about the importance of knowing who you are. What are you up to these days? I just completed writing a book, "Action Has No Season." It's about understanding the complexities of gaining wealth and authority. From my perspective, one can only survive if one works. The book was written in large measure for my children. From a business standpoint, why is it important to know yourself? You might have a deal that has a business plan based on empirical knowledge — this plan works, and this one doesn't. But then comes this carnal knowledge, what old folks would call gut or mother wit or instinct, that says, 'I can make this work even though on paper it's marginal.' Or, 'It looks great on paper, but I don't feel this is something I can do or want to do.' Well, that's vision. If you can get in touch with what you understand to be your natural abilities, and you blend that with academic training, then you have what I define as a formula for success. What is still on your to-do list? Legacy building is an important component in my life. If 100 years ago, Henry Ford had been an African-American and his culture would have been to hire people who looked a lot like him, how many millions of people in the past 100 years, who are now described as poor, would have made a living, educated their kids? What would this country look like if Rockefeller had been black? What would this country be like after 100 years of having a woman or a Hispanic at the head of major companies? My legacy, I hope, would be to put in place a number of companies that might be able to employ people who, in the status quo of the old-boy network, would have been excluded. . . . And I don't mean diversity the way they flip the word around, because it's a token here, and then these people don't even stay. . . . You hear the chatter of diversity, but the reality is you still don't have access to capital. Do you and Steve have separate areas of expertise? Or is everything a joint decision? It's a combination of both. I think Steve would probably call me the visionary in the company, the one who tends to guide. I started the company in '74 — this is an anniversary. Steve is our chief operating officer, so he has the lion's share responsibility of overseeing the parts. That's the synergy that leads to the legacy. Did you have a sense of being very imaginative as a kid? When I was young I was a business person. I had a landscape company. Most kids called it cutting grass. I also had an auto spa. Most kids called it washing cars. One of the things I would do is define myself. I prefer to define myself (rather) than have someone else define me. Here's an example. Steve and I were given an Entrepreneur of the Year Award by The (St. Louis) American. Malcolm Briggs introduces us. He says, "Ladies and gentlemen —

the Donald Trumps of St. Louis, Mike and Steve Roberts." Steve speaks and he thanks everybody. We do our little barb between each other, about how he's the better-looking and I say he's jealous because my mother favored me and I have hair and he doesn't. Then I say, "And Malcolm, by the way, let me correct you for the future. We are not the Donald Trumps of St. Louis. Donald Trump is the Roberts Brothers of New York." People came out of their seats. Frequently, I hear young people say, "I want to move to another city." I say to them, does the other city have asphalt, sidewalks, McDonald's, airports, cars, gasoline stations? What's different between one city and the next? It's not a geographic thing; it's a mental change you have to deal with. You have to see yourself and define yourself inside of your environment. And they say, "Well, you have homes in the Bahamas and you're developing in Nassau and whatever." Yeah, but this is my core, my base. Why not work where your base is strongest, where your contacts are in place and you can establish your future based on perhaps a legacy that your parents or theirs have built? With my children coming up, my vision is that there is a legacy to be built and they have responsibilities to our community to help develop our people — and I mean all the people in our community. And if they are at all confused, I tell them that inheritance is not a birthright, it is a privilege. . . . The privilege is predicated on your level of community work, business development and being good kids.

And knock on wood, they are good kids. Any hankering to go back into politics? There's a difference between rich and powerful, and wealth and authority. If rich screams, wealth whispers. Wealth is the stable rock that the rich are trying to attain. Power flees. Authority controls power. I know you're a big donator to political campaigns. I am. So there's the authority. Politicians have the power. I have the authority. As a businessman and an African-American are your political leanings split between the parties? I think most of the candidates we see from both parties are really OK people. If the person can win, that's the important consideration. Too frequently people go out on an emotional, philosophical level. As a capitalist, you're about winning. And as a former politician and now a statesman, one thing you always remember is how to count. =====================

MICHAEL ROBERTS Chairman and chief executive, the Roberts Cos. Age: 55 Education: bachelor of science degree in English literature, communications, Lindenwood College, 1971; law degree, St. Louis University School of Law, 1974 Personal: Lives in the Central West End; married to Jeanne; twins Michael Jr. and Jeanne, 25; Fallon, 22; Meaghan, 19 Career highlights: Founded Roberts-Roberts & Associates with brother Steve, 1974; St. Louis Board of Aldermen, 19771985; launched Roberts Broadcasting Co, 1989, as licensee for Channel 46; founded Roberts Wireless Communications, 1998; recent real estate investments include Roberts Plaza and Roberts Village in north St. Louis, the Roberts Mayfair hotel, American Theatre.

NEWSPOINTS

B.E. 100S

Roberts Brothers Cash In Big On Alamosa Deal Sale provides revenue to purchase upscale hotels across the country

By Glenn Townes

Siblings Michael Roberts Sr. and Steven Roberts Sr., owners of Roberts Cos., based in St. Louis, netted more than $100 million on the sale of their shares in Alamosa Holdings Inc. the nation's largest Sprint PCS affiliate, in February.

Initially, the brothers were among Alamosa's largest shareholders, arising out of a 2001 merger between Alamosa and Roberts Wireless Co. This merger yielded the Roberts brothers an 11% stake in publicly held Alamosa-or 11.4 million shares of stock worth more than $380 million at the time.

After five years of gradually liquidating portions of their holdings, the Roberts brothers sold the balance of their shares at $18.75, owing to a friendly takeover by Sprint Nextel. The total proceeds roughly $112.5 million-will allow the family-owned business "to make even more opportunistic deals," according to Michael Roberts Sr., chairman and chief executive of the company. "My brother and I plan to increase the value of our family assets to more than a billion dollars by 2008."

Roberts says funds acquired from the sale have been used to purchase upscale hotels across the country, including the first African American-owned luxury hotel and conference center in Atlanta, the Crowne Plaza Marietta/Atlanta, which they purchased and renovated for $9.1 million.

"In selling our wireless phone company, my brother and I are expanding our financial interests to include the hospitality industry," Roberts says. Due to recent forays into the industry by black businessmen such as former BET kingpin Bob Johnson, Roberts hopes African Americans will begin to realize the tremendous business opportunity that exists in the hospitality business.

Roberts says hotels were recently purchased in St. Louis; Tampa, Florida; and Houston in private/franchise deals. They will be managed separately from all of their other business interests.

"We also want to continue to grow our existing business entities," Roberts says, including their urban shopping centers, television stations, and Bahamas real estate investments.

The Roberts Cos. is a multifaceted enterprise containing a myriad of entrepreneurial endeavors, including a group of five hotels and conference centers, urban shopping centers, office buildings, residential developments, a management consulting firm, America's eighth largest broadcast and telecommunications tower company, and an aviation company.

MISSOURI
MEETINGS & EVENTS

$5.00
SPRING 2005

THE ROBERTS BROTHERS

by Kevin M. Mitchell

Two of the Gateway City's Most Successful Siblings

Expand into the Hospitality Industry

"Can you believe they like each other so much, and yet they are brothers?"

Michael Jennings jokes of his bosses, Mike and Steve Roberts. Jennings, general manager of the Roberts Orpheum Theater (formerly the American Theater), is laughing, but it's true. Of the many aspects that are impressive about the brothers—their upbringing, their days in politics, and their ascent into the upper echelon of entrepreneurship—is how comfortable they are with each other. For this interview, the busy duo were gracious hosts in their artfully furnished office of the Victor Roberts building, despite the constant buzzing of their cell phones. It became an inadvertent tag-team match, with one brother starting a thought, then apologizing for having to take a call, followed by the other brother seamlessly finishing the sentence. But they are a team to be reckoned with.

They've been awarded the Mayor's Spirit of St. Louis Award, among many other honors, having invested more than $15 million in development projects in the north-central part of St. Louis. They also own a construction management and consulting firm, as well as a television broadcasting property. And their reach goes far beyond St. Louis: older brother Steve just returned from the Bahamas, where they are building a 50-condominium development in a gated community.

One of their recent acquisitions is the historic Mayfair Hotel, now called the Roberts Mayfair, and the theater next door, formerly the American, now the Roberts Orpheum Theater. They have once again invested in older properties in St. Louis that have seen better days. But head and heart equally guide business decisions. They see a future that's both profitable and good for the community.

"So much is great about this place," Jennings says, standing on the stage of the theater. He then points to the opera boxes and tells about a recent wedding that put the band up there and the bride and groom's table on stage. "It's so flexible for meetings, events, shows—anything, really. It's a great old building." He points out the improvements that have been made, and he hopes to have more done. Later that day he'll meet with the brothers to see if there's a way to update the bar and the bathrooms, an expensive proposition. And they hope to have a grand opening sometime in the spring, even though the facility is being used already with great success.

Unbroken Chain of Responsibility

As young boys growing up in north St. Louis, the brothers would walk three bustling blocks from their house to find themselves in the crowded Sears building, never knowing that one day they would own the property.

"It's where we bought swimming trunks," Mike tells. "And they'd have roasted nuts that smelled so good."

But they would see their neighborhood slide into abandoned buildings, including the Sears building. Business leaders and politicians gave up on the area. But it's inspiring that the brothers would one day aim some of their revitalization efforts at that very building, then see it re-open with dozens of businesses and become the headquarters to many of their own businesses. (They renamed it the Victor Roberts Building in honor of their father.)

"It is satisfying to come back to your own neighborhood and have marketable changes occur," Mike said. "It is rewarding to see jobs being created, and it's great to see these businesses come in and succeed. We consider them our partners in this redevelopment."

What gave them a huge head start were parents who instilled a strong work ethic in them at an early age, as well as their participation in household chores, which began what they call an "unbroken chain of responsibility."

"We were never poor, we just never had any money," Mike says about their years growing up. "But our mother made it a point to expose us to different kinds of cultural events. We would go to the theater, including the American."

But while other kids were just cutting grass, they ran a lawn service. While others merely washed cars, they had an Auto Spot car cleaning service.

Older brother Mike would go to college and law school, with Steve following him. Then came work in real estate before both became city aldermen in the late 1970s and bounded into the highly contentious fray that is St. Louis city politics. Their interest in the hospitality industry grew out of their days as aldermen.

"When we were aldermen, we learned that in order for St. Louis to have a significant and robust downtown, we needed to have convention business," Steve says. "But we didn't have enough hotel rooms, and that became the proverbial chicken or the egg— which needs to come first? So we thought St. Louis first had to build that convention center."

"The next step was getting enough hotel rooms," Mike continues. "Despite the fact that St. Louis had a large convention center, the big conventions were reluctant to come here because of the lack of rooms."

The brothers have taken over the Mayfair, a 182-suite hotel that is aimed at the upper end of the market.

"It has very nice amenities, like you'd find in a New York City boutique hotel," Mike says. They are hoping to attract CEOs and other executives who would prefer a hotel like the Mayfair to a larger one. [And it has a great history—see sidebar.] As charming as the Mayfair is, no amount of renovation would solve one problem: the lack of a big room. The Mayfair has several small meeting rooms, three of which open onto the beautiful mezzanine, but nothing that could adequately host

hundreds. So the brothers eyed the underused American Theater next door.

It's understandable that the old theater would appeal to them, and not just because their mother took them to cultural events there. The theater began life owned by two other brothers, Charles and Louis Cella. Opened in 1917, it was a an outlet of the Vaudeville circuit under the "Orpheum" franchise. When Vaudeville died out and movies came in, it became a movie house. In the second half of the last century, it became a roadhouse for all kinds of acts before hosting punk bands. (Jennings points to a filled-in orchestra pit and explains that that was done so punkers could have an adequate "mosh" pit.)

Sprucing Up the New Venue

"We have a three-fold plan for it," Steve explains. "One, we want to provide a traditional theater to be used for smaller concerts. Second, we want to bring in cultural groups such as ballet troupes. "Third, it'll be used for weddings and corporate events. We have eight to 10 weddings [booked] already, and it's a very dramatic place for [those events]. They can set up big tables for dinner and seat 400 people easily. For a more Las Vegas-style event, with cocktail tables, you can set up for

as many as 900. Stadium theaterstyle seating can hold more than 1,500."

But can St. Louis support another facility like this? "Let me answer that question in historical terms," Mike says. "Up to the 1950s, St. Louis had more theaters than almost any other city in

America, second only to New York. And in the years since then, we've lost about every one of them. Going back further, to 1904, there were more millionaires here than in New York. We're still a major player in many ways, and can be again." What the brothers find encouraging is the fact that these two facilities are out of the ordinary.

"The hotel's right there, and the rooms have these beautiful ceilings and chandeliers. You can see why we decided to bring it back. And the outside of the building is quite literally art." And they have ambitious ideas—already they are interested in taking advantage of the "Final Four" basketball tournament in St. Louis in March. They have been in discussion with big names like Nike to take advantage of the facility.

In and Out of the Rule Book

The Robertses are in a unique position to be especially effective cheerleaders for the St. Louis hospitality industry: Mike is chairman of the board of the National Association of Black Hotel Owners, Operators and Developers, and the Roberts Mayfair is currently the only African American-owned convention hotel in the U.S. "And of all the thousands of hotels in this country, only 24 are wholly owned by African Americans—and another 48 have some African American ownership—so we are pioneers in that respect," he says.

He adds that when you think of all the minorities who travel, all the black fraternities who put on events, including organizations such as the Southern Baptists, there's a lot of impact to be gained from the Robertses' unique position. "The corporate philosophies of a lot of companies, including Anheuser-Busch, the May Co. and SBC, are aimed at doing business with African American-we're in a unique position to say, 'Come here.'"

But first and foremost, he's pro-St. Louis, and is interested in using "every element in and out of the rule book to bring people here." One of the challenges they face is that of perception. Both agree that outside the Midwest, St. Louis is looked upon as having a conservative bent, as not being "hip." That's a notion they are trying to dispel, and it needs to happen through promotion. Steve points out that Memphis a few years ago was nothing. "Then, boom—someone just came in and made up Beale Street." "We're not exploiting our resources," Mike adds. Steve thinks St. Louis can do better at attracting convention business. "Does it take Mike and me sitting in a room with other players? Maybe it would make sense to have a subset of advisers, people from the downtown business community, to encourage business to come to St. Louis—a source that says, 'Let us help market this community.'

"We're not saying that those doing it aren't talented, we're just wondering if there's a better way to market St. Louis and Missouri. We get comfortable with who we are while places like Indianapolis and Pittsburgh are beating us up pretty good. They seem to be better organized." He adds that the state's tourism groups could be more cooperative.

"From my point of view, it's not St. Louis vs. Kansas City vs. Branson," he says. "We are all in this together."

As an alderman, Steve says he sponsored "about every major development legislation there was, including Laclede's Landing, Union Station and many others. It was funny because back then,

Indianapolis, Cleveland, and Pittsburgh people were coming here and saying, 'Wow!' But now they've passed us up! They didn't stand still. They were always moving." But what's most important is being able to look squarely in the face of those who book conventions and say, "Come here," the brothers say. Yes, it's an investment that isn't going to yield immediate dividends, but they are patient, and even think it'll be 2009 before they get the size convention they believe St. Louis deserves.

Despite all their success, when asked what it takes to be a great leader, they are modest. "We don't see ourselves as leaders, only public servants," Steve says. "We see everything about our business, our partnerships, as serving the community. People might need to find a description for it, but our view is that we're just part of the community, doing our part to make it a better place."

(Kevin Mitchell is a frequent contributor from St. Louis, Mo.)

The Mayfair: Historic Property The Mayfair opened in 1925 and was one of the city's premier hospitality venues for most of its life. John Barrymore, Douglas Fairbanks, Cary Grant, Harry S. Truman, Tallulah Bankhead, Bernadette Peters and Lou Rawls are just a few of the celebrities who stayed there through the years.

German-born Charles Heiss was hired to run the Statler Hotel but left after seven years to realize his dream of owning his own hotel, the Mayfair, which he put up right next door to the Statler. Construction began in 1924 on the 18-story hotel. It features ornate cornice work, beading and Italian-style urns. Four hundred rooms had private baths, and uniformed
operators piloted the three highspeed elevators, which were manually operated until the mid-1990s.

KMOX Radio opened its first studio in 1925 in a two-room suite in the hotel. Visitors could watch radio broadcasts. In the summer of 1967, the Mayfair opened a rooftop swimming pool—the first of its kind in St. Louis. (The Roberts brothers are hoping to reopen it this year.) By 1970, the hotel had lost its luster and was sold. It went through various hands, closed in 1987 for $20 million in renovation, and reopened in 1990 with 184 luxury suites. Today the Roberts brothers own it and contract with the Wyndham hotel group to run it.

St. Louis Magazine
Brothers, Who Art Thou?

June 2006
Michael and Steven Roberts built a broadcasting empire and a bricks-and-mortar empire, and now they're buying hotels. They're smart and nice and dedicated family men. So why can't they shake their critics?

By Susan C. Thomson

Worshipers stand and sway, offering up arms and hallelujahs to the exuberant accompaniment of an electric guitar and keyboard. For the first half hour or so of this Sunday service, Faith Miracle Temple in Florissant rocks. The collection follows, settling the whipped-up congregation down a bit for this morning's inspirational speaker.

Enter, to a standing ovation, Michael Victor Roberts, chairman and chief executive of the St. Louis–based Roberts Companies, more than 60 different businesses that add up to one of the country's largest black-owned enterprises, worth half a billion dollars, give or take a few million.

Roberts—with heavy-lidded blue eyes and a feathering of white in what was an Afro when he burst on the scene as a St. Louis alderman a generation ago—ambles up to the altar. In a fine blue suit that conforms perfectly to his frame, disguising a slight thickness in the middle these days, he looks every bit the "cold-blooded capitalist" he jokingly calls himself.

Cordless mike in his right hand, he holds forth casually for nearly 45 minutes with no notes. As a public speaker he's a natural, relaxed and engaged. Though he has given versions of this talk any number of times already and knows exactly where to pause for emphasis or a laugh, he varies the presentation each time. And, while always making it sound spontaneous, he always manages to work in certain key points:

On growing up in St. Louis, son of a father who worked as a night supervisor for the U.S. Postal Service: "We weren't rich people. We weren't poor people. We just never had any money."

On his company's Donald Trump–like penchant for slapping the family name on its buildings: "People say, 'You have a big ego problem.' I say, 'You have a big envy problem.'"

On the difference between the rich and the wealthy: "Rich people scream; wealthy people whisper."

On the difference between power and authority: "Power eludes; authority endures ... Romans had power; Jesus had authority."

Talks such as these are Cliffs Notes versions of Action Has No Season: Strategies and Secrets to Gaining Wealth and Authority, an advice book Roberts published last year. The book and the speeches are, he says, his philanthropy, his giving back, his legacy. At 57, he has reached a summit and a summing-up point in an extraordinary, ongoing career.

Actually, it's been half of a joint career with his younger brother Steven Craig Roberts, 54, the companies' president and chief operating officer. Together, the brothers have prospered spectacularly from a revolving portfolio of timely investments in television stations, including UPN Channel 46 in St. Louis, wireless communications, cell phone towers, aviation and, more and more over the years, real estate. "They are hard-driven, hardcore business-men," says one of their peers, "and they have amassed an amazing amount of money. It's a helluva Horatio Alger story."

Or, as Michael likes to say, not bad for a couple of inner-city kids from St. Louis. Street kids they weren't, though. They were raised by caring parents in what he describes as a "very Ozzie and Harriet" way, taught to play sports, do well in school and earn some of their own spending money. They lived in a large, lovely ranch-style house in the Penrose neighborhood, in a cul-de-sac developed with young black families in mind—but surrounded by blue collar Irish and Italian neighbors e were playing with a neighborhood kid in our big back yard when I was about 6," Steve recalls, "and his father, a big-bellied guy you might call a redneck, called the kid home, saying, 'I don't want you playing with those niggers."

Steve ran inside to ask his mom what a nigger was, "Just remember, "she told him after explaining, "that if someone doesn't want to play with you, it's not your fault."

The message stuck for life.

205

The brothers cut grass and washed cars for extra cash as teenagers, and they scored their first big grown-up deal in 1982, when they rescued an abandoned former Sears store at Kingshighway and Martin Luther King and named it the Victor Roberts Building, for their father. A few years ago, they developed a strip shopping center set back from  the street behind the former store and christened it Roberts Village. "We are looking to probably double the size of it in the next three years," says

Steven. "We've been in touch with a couple large national retailers who say they're changing their urban perspective. Retailers are starting to understand how many consumer dollars the city drives out every day."

For now, the neighborhood remains downscale. Still, the brothers insist, it's their neighborhood, the place they grew up. Hence their deliberate decision to locate Channel 46 and their corporate headquarters here, alongside the payday-loan office, the tax-preparation service, the nail salon and the cheap eateries and clothing shops that are among their tenants.

This proves, they say, that success hasn't spoiled them, a claim echoed by Frederic Steinbach, an advertising executive who has known Steven and Michael Roberts professionally and socially for years. "I don't see anything different about the way they treat people now than they did 25 years ago," he says.

But what a difference a tad over a mile of Kingshighway has made in their scale and style of life. They live now at its intersection with Lindell Boulevard, in a grand neighborhood they remember walking by wid eyed as boys. Here, a block apart, Michael built a custom home and Steven bought a historic one. They also have two houses near condominiums they developed in the Bahamas. Steven bought in Southern Illinois with the intention of building there, and Michael owns recreational property near Cuba, Mo., as well as a condo in Malibu. "Now, when we talk about doing something, it's within the realm of possibility," says Steven. "I don't know that there's anything we can't frankly."

Steven and Michael. Michael and Steven. The names are spoken in the same breath, almost as if they were identical twins. From the superficiality of distance, it's easy to see them that way. Both have law degrees—Michael from Saint Louis University, Steven from Washington University. Both were political wunderkind, elected to the St. Louis Board of Aldermen in their twenties and eventually running for may (Michael in 1989, Steven in 1993). They sound enough alike that a receptionist can't distinguish their voices on the phone, and they ar to share certain qualities of character.

Former St. Louis Mayor Vincent Schoemehl remembers them from their aldermanic days as sensible. "They weren't get-in the way guys," he says. "You could approach them with a reasonable proposition and get a reasonable response."

Smart but not condescending, confident but not overbearing-they strike the right balance again and again as I spend time with them, beginning with a joint interview in their third-floor offices in the Victor Roberts Building.

Their father works here, in his namesake building, as does their baby sister, Lori, who is vice president for development. The youngest Robe brother, Mark, 47, left a few years ago to forge his own destiny in Colorado.

The building has three entrances, each with a conspicuous sign on the doors announcing that concealed weapons are not allowed inside. In the Roberts' reception area, a TV is tuned to Channel 46, and the walls are crowded with plaques, diplomas, citations, news articles and photographs with various dignitaries, including Jimmy Carter Charles, Prince of Wales.

Michael receives me in his office, which is filled with African art, but we are interrupted almost immediately by his cell phone, which he takes into the hall to talk. As I page through magazines about luxury cars, I overhear words such as "million" and "dollars." or Steven tells me later that his brother has been fascinated by cars since he acquired a "fixer-upper" Triumph TR3 as a college sophomore and that the half dozen or so he owns now include an Aston Martin, a Mercedes- Benz coupe and a Rolls-Royce. Each brother drives a Ford Expedition as his everyday car.

Michael returns from his call and takes the sofa, leaning back, hands free. Steven—cherubic, hairline receding—arrives, a sheaf of papers in his hand, and sits erect in a chair. Their separate postures hint at a crucia difference between them, one that becomes even clearer as Steven multitasks, now studying his papers, now looking up over his reading glasses to join a conversation that his brother is doing his best to steer.

Whereas steven merely outgoing, Michael comes on as a thorough extrovert. They're less mirror images of each other than subtly complementary personalities, as no one knows better than their Victor, their company's chief financial officer. "Michael's the visionary," Victor says. "He goes out and initiates things. Steven pulls everything together. He's the glue."

Michael the big-picture guy, Steven the detail man-the brothers say they've been playing these roles since childhood. "Steve as a child was very inquiring person, very intelligent, the one my parents expected to get things done," says Michael. "I would be the one to find excuses." Steven agrees; he refers fondly to his brothers as the dreamer and deal-maker. To be with the two brothers together is to sense an extraordinarily tight bond between them. "Steve and I ...," begins Michael. "Mike and I ...," begins Steven. For public occasions, they've perfected a teasing shtick in which Steven claims to be better looking and Michael ripostes that he has more hair.

Eventually the interview, like nearly every conversation with the Roberts brothers, gets around to family. They want me and anybody else who will listen to know they are third-generation St. Louisans, grandsons of a physician on one side and an engineer on the other. They are descendants of blacks and whites, slaves and small landowner families are extraordinarily tight, gathering at Steven's house every Thanksgiving and Fourth of July and, along with several dozen family friends, at Michael's house every Christmas to feast on duck, turkey, chitlins, ribs, chicken, salads, mashed and sweet potatoes and vegetables—much of it prepared by Michael himself. Michael is cook, Steven says. Ditto for Steven, according to Michael. Both credit their mother, Delores, for teaching them.

They talk freely-except about the business up and downs they surely have weathered these many years. They say they've learned some lessons. Discussion closed. "Failure" is not in their vocabulary. They speak fearlessly of "risk," a big chunk of which they've assumed with bold purchases these last three years of the Mayfair Hotel, the American Theatre and the former St. Louis Public Schools headquarters—now, respectively, the Roberts Mayfair Hotel, the Roberts Orpheum Theater and the Roberts Lofts on the Plaza. Coming soon to these same up-and coming two square blocks bounded by Locust, St. Charles, Eighth and 10th streets downtown: the Roberts Tower, a 24story residential-retail office complex.

Big stuff for a paid who, as Steven says, "haven't always had banks buy into our vision." They had to dig into their own pockets for $4 million to develop Roberts Village. Not that they're averse to debt: "My definition of a millionaire is one who can borrow a million dollars," Michael says. The bankers must be coming around, though: Two of them are waiting in the reception area as I leave.

The Roberts brothers allow themselves no downtime between deals. These days, it's hotels, a whole new venture for them. Since buying two in Houston and one in Atlanta earlier this year, they've been prowling the country for more.

"The hospitality industry now is where broadcast TV was in the '90s," says Steven.

"Under-valued," adds Michael.

Otherwise, what do they know about the industry?

"As much as we knew about TV stations and wireless," Michael says. In other words, not all that much.

But enough to succeed.

Racially, though to a lesser degree than economically, Michael and Steven Roberts have broken through in St. Louis. They were among first African Americans admitted to the Missouri Athletic Club. (Although, since buying the Mayfair Hotel, they have let their memberships lapse; why pay a fee to the competition?) They were al admitted to the historically racist Veiled Prophet Society, a fact that did not endear them to the black community at the time, according to a fellow African-American member.

Now that the brothers have become "filthy frickin'rich," some African Americans "would like to see them use their political and economic capital on behalf of the disenfranchised population on whose backs t really built their empire," says Antonio D. French, a black activist and journalist who operates the political blog pubdefweekly.com. "Not everyone thinks they are saints. Many people think they play both s of the fence politically and don't take stands on much of anything. Many people would like to see them do even more with their North St. Louis property in the way of reinvestment. Many people would like to see them use their 'Black PAC' for something more than leverage in statewide political campaigns."

Steven listens to the charges calmly. "We are, of course, Democrats," he says. "We support candidates, Republican or Democrat, who we think can do the best for our community— and we do that nationwide. We hosted two fundraisers for Barack Obama before anybody in St. Louis knew about him." He draws a deep breath. "First off, you can't criticize someone who is the only one doing anything. We are the model. We're the ones saying, 'Please come and do more along with us.' And we have been saying that for 25 years, and still no one has come. There's a lot more we can do, but we would rather not do it by ourselves."

Black activist Percy Green finds "a certain amount of selfishness" in the Roberts' aloofness, and what he sees as their failure to acknowledge and help "people in the streets putting pressure on for change." A well-known black executive bristles at this criticism: "How do we know what they are giving away? That's their business. Sure, they used the minority angle to get started, and they found good opportunities and did a damn good job of exploiting them. That's capitalism."

Steven says, "We have always allowed anyone with an interest in presenting their view to the community to come on air. No other TV station in this market allows that. And look at the diversity of our tenants. We have a sickle-cell organization, we have the Nation of Some folks say, 'Why are you associated with an inflammatory organization?' They're a great tenant, and the forgotten few are brought up because of Minister Farrakhan and his organization. When people wanted to go to the Million Man March, they were organized in this building. So our response is, 'Tell us who does more than we do.'"

The brothers part company in one way: Michael serves on the boards of no St. Louis nonprofits, whereas Steven serves on so many that, to jog hi memory, he has to ask an assistant for his résumé. This in hand, he checks off, among others, the Regional Business Council, the Black

Leadership Roundtable, the Muny, the Repertory Theatre of St. Louis, the Missouri Historical Society, the St. Louis Sports Commission, the foundations of Children's and BJC hospitals. He also chairs the board MERS/Missouri Goodwill Industries and is vice chairman of the board of Logan College of Chiropractic.

The Roberts brothers and establishment St.Louis have met and shaken hands—but the relationship stops short of an embrace."

"They love that Roberts name, they've got it on everything.

Wouldn't surprise me if they ran again. They don't strike me as people who leave things undone."

Nor, however, do they suck up.

"We've always been outsiders," Steven says, and Michael quickly amends the statement: "We've been trailblazers."

The brothers have never belonged to Civic Progress, that booster organization made up of St. Louis' top CEOs, nor to any St. Louis corporate boards or country clubs. Never been asked, they say.

Michael sent his four children through the Clayton public schools under the voluntary St. Louis city-county deseg program. Steven's three children were also in Clayton schools until administrative turmoil prompted a switch. After research, he and his wife chose Whitfield in Creve Coeur, not John Burroughs or MICDS. "My sense of those other schools is that there is something of a caste system there," Steven says. "We fight those categories."

Steven Roberts Jr. is bound for Miami University this fall; his younger brother and sister will be at Whitfield. Michael's youngest, Meaghan, goes to Pepperdine University, where her sister Fallon is a law student and his oldest, twins Jeanne and Michael Jr., 27, received their law degrees. Michael Jr. recently left Armstrong Teasdale to join the family business.

At the church, his father holds the audience rapt.

On thinking outside the box: "For you to be thinking outside the box, you have to be in a box ... There is no box ... There's nothing for you to think outside of." On time management: "Eighty-six thousand four hundred seconds are given you every day ... Live every moment to the fullest."

On priorities: "Family first."

As he talks, laughter and applause-and the occasional "amen" or "that's right"—ripple through the audience. Roberts concludes with a well-honed exhortation: "Let's change the old-boy network to the homeboy network and go out and make some money.

The congregation leaps to its feet, clapping.

Speeches

"The Greatest Time in History to Be in Business"

Speech to Black Advertising & Marketing Professionals

September 21, 1995

It is my pleasure to come before you today.

As your speaker, I am challenged once again to come up with a subject matter that is relevant, helpful, and educational.

I'm here because the Million Man March made me realize that I have a responsibility to share my knowledge and experience with the larger community of African
 Americans —to do whatever I can to help my brothers and sisters grow and succeed in business and in our society.
Thus, my mission here today is to describe what I believe is the road to success and prosperity, and, hope that I will inspire some of you to strive for success and use that success to help others as I hope to help you today.

I am still, and will always be, a student of business. I have learned that the business world and the opportunities it brings are never static...both are always changing. I have learned to change with it...to recognize emerging opportunities and seize them whenever possible. Today, I would like to share some of my knowledge and experience with you, and discuss what I believe the future can offer to those who have the vision to recognize change and the courage to pursue their vision.

It is my belief that the american dream is for everyone. And, it's through the free enterprise system that the dream will come true. I'm certain you've all heard this before, and the lingering unanswered question is: "How do I recognize those opportunities that will lead to success?"

I'm going to begin my answer with a short history lesson. You've heard people say that history repeats itself. I believe this is true, but not in the way most people perceive the repetition. Let's examine our current history for a moment.

The 1960s and 1970s were a time of great social change in America...the emergence and institutionalization of the civil rights movement. This change resulted in great numbers of blacks being elected to political office and succeeding in business and the professions.

Then, just as it appeared we were making real progress, the 1980s witnessed the beginning of a fundamental change in our economy...the beginning of the end of our industrial/manufacturing economy. More and more of our traditional industries lost their dominant position...American textile, automobile, electronic and oil industries could not compete in the emerging global economy.

The equal employment opportunities we fought so hard to secure began to appear as shallow victories in the face of massive layoffs and dying industries.

Now, let's look back one hundred years. What do we find? The 1860s and the 1870s were decades of great social change...the initial emergence and institutionalization of the civil rights movement. Reconstruction witnessed historic numbers of blacks elected to political office. In fact, during this period, blacks comprised a majority of the lower chamber of South Carolina's state legislature.

Although still physically segregated, blacks excelled in business and the professions as never before.

This all began to change in the 1880s. As, just like the 1980s, wealth began to accumulate at the top, the "robber barons" became the driving force of the economy, and great masses of people were economically dislocated. Fear led to the growth of the Klu Klux Klan and civil rights were curtailed.

But, it was also the decade in which America abandoned its agrarian social and economic structure and became a full fledged industrial society. The 1890s through the early 1900s was an entrepreneur's dream time.

1899: Thomas Edison built the first electric power plant in New york and John D. Rockefeller formed Standard Oil Company.

1903: Henry Ford began mass production of the gas engine automobile.

1908: The model-T Ford made automobile transportation affordable for middle class americans.

You didn't have to be a Henry Ford or a Rockefeller to prosper in this environment. The visionary entrepreneur of the 1890s-1900s would have looked at the model-T and recognized a fortune in the manufacture of tires, steel, and even piping for automobile seat covers!

He or she would have looked at the growing use of Edison's

light bulb and the ability to distribute electric power to masses of people and recognized a fortune in the design and manufacture of lamps!

What have we learned from this brief history lesson? We've learned that we are in a comparable period of change and opportunity. The 1990s and the beginning decades of the twenty-first century are America's change from an Industrial society to an Information society.

This change will be most notable in the fields of communications and transportation, but it will also change our family structures, our work habits and environments, our educational system, and of course, our economy.

If we could resurrect an 1890s entrepreneur, he or she would look at this emerging information age and see countless opportunities in the distribution of information, in the development of new ways to communicate an idea and market a product. The emerging wireless communications industry will propel these opportunities to a global scale.

And, if you think globally....this about this...

- Fifty percent of the world's population has never made a telephone call;

- But, one of the most sophisticated telephone networks in the world is in **Rwanda**, where 100% of the main phone lines are digital. In the U.S., 49% of the main phone lines are digital.

- The world's developing countries – in South America, Asia, and Africa – plan to spend $200 billion in the next five years to bring their phone networks—and their populations— into the twenty-first century.

- AT&T had fewer than 100 people stationed abroad a decade ago; today, they have 50,000 employees overseas.

And, remember, you don't have to be in Africa to do business there. That's the essence of the information age.

Look   at the emerging information age market in the us:

- In 1994, PC sales exceeded TV sales for the first time ever.

- In 2000, PC makers will be looking at a potential market of 106 million households.

- Or, consider Intel – the premier maker of computer chips – growing at better than 30% a year, many market analysts expect the chip maker to overtake Ford and Exxon as the nation's profit leader within 10 years.

- One of the most profound changes in this country will come as a result of the new telecommunications bill passed by Congress just last week. It's the industry's equivalent of the Berlin Wall coming down. In essence, the bill will sweep away regulatory barriers that prevent telephone, cable, broadcast and other communications companies from entering each other's markets.

- The combination of new wireless communications technology and the new telecommunications law will create over one million new jobs by the year 2005.

- As the nation's communications market expands, many economists expect it to affect job growth much as the interstate highway system spurred growth not just in the auto industry, but in cities and towns nationwide.

And, we must understand that we are not at the beginning of this change. We are in the middle of the first major wave of change. A most compelling example is Forbes Magazine current list of "America's Richest People". Nine of the top fifty fortunes have been made in computer software or hardware. Bill Gates, the founder of Microsoft, is the most famous of these. One of the top fifty is in communications....McCaw cellular. The Rockefellers, Fords, and Mellons are still there, but they no longer lead the pack.

Just think for a minute about the change that's occurred during the past five years. How many of you were computer literate at age seven? Or age five? The majority of today's seven and five year olds will not know what it's like to be computer illiterate. Information technology is a staple of their environment.

This is, in my opinion, the greatest time in history to be in business. It is a time when vision and the right ideas can lead to great success, wealth and fortune. Let's re-visit our history lesson. The 1860s and 1870s were a time of great social progress for African-Americans, as were the 1960s and 1970s. During these times, black power was, indeed black! The 1880s and 1890s were a time of great prosperity for African-Americans. The 1990s and beyond can witness the same progress, and you can be part of this progress. In

1996, my friends, black power is green!

I believe African-Americans have everything we need right now to achieve true economic equality. African-Americans generate three hundred billion dollars in income each year. You and I represent the **fourteenth largest economy in the industrialized world**.

Let me give you some examples:

- There are now thirteen million African-Americans employed in the country, nearly half of them in professional and technical positions in the business world.

- There are 425,000 black-owned businesses in the country.

· The top black owned business is TLC Beatrice International Holdings, a New York based food processor and distributor with annual revenues of $1.6 billion.

Yes, there are millions of blacks who are still impoverished. But, other millions have been successful not only as individuals who have survived slavery, segregation, and American apartheid, but as an enduring race of people who scientists say developed highly complex and sophisticated civilizations in Africa long before the white man evolved on the European continent. In other words, more than we have ever acknowledged, success is a tradition in our race.

. Johnson publishing of Chicago, a publishing, broadcasting, and cosmetics empire founded by John H. Johnson, has annual sales of $270 million.

. Among the newer black -owned businesses is Threads 4 Life of Los Angeles, which makes the Cross Colours clothing line that features positive messages of peace, racial harmony, and black pride printed in vibrant colors. Though only a few years old, Threads 4 Life has sales in excess of $89 million annually.

How do you join the successful millions?

Have you ever noticed how excited and creative you get when you really go after something you want? My mind goes into overtime in those situations. I solve minor problems in my sleep. My focus is so intense, even my dreams become energized. And, when you are that energized, you draw people to you who empower you further.

You must start with an agenda. I can see a lot of people right now saying to themselves, "I don't have an agenda!". I believe you do, but perhaps you don't realize it. An agenda is the means by which you reach your goals. Without an agenda, you are like a ship without a rudder, a tourist without a map.

Your personal agenda should be like the spray of a hose: The more focused it is, the more powerful. With a focused agenda in mind, you can concentrate your energy, enthusiasm, and excitement on your goals. Let me give you a few strategies for setting your agenda and focusing on it:

- Set priorities for your agenda and go public with them.
- List those things you have to offer: Your expertise, talents, ideas, and resources.

If you can't articulate your agenda and goals to others, then you have not really defined them.

I expect you are now asking yourself, "once I have an agenda, how do I get into the system? How do I succeed and prosper in this rapidly changing environment?"

First, you must recognize that powerful forces will do everything possible to maintain the "status quo". And, the current "status quo" overwhelmingly benefits the white male. They make the rules and they control the game. But, the game is changing and they will inevitably fail to recognize this change. In a decade or so, their rules won't matter because they won't fit the game.

This is your opportunity to create the system...to write the rules of the game...if you have the vision to understand how the new game will be played.

Robert Reich, president Clinton's Secretary of Labor, has studied this change and determined that the rules will be established within a global, not national, economy and by small groups of entrepreneurs who develop the skill and ability to: (1) recognize a need; (2) fill the need; (3) and broker their ideas or products to those who demonstrate the need. He envisions the new global economy as comprised of large multi-national corporations and "webs" of small entrepreneurial businesses that serve their evolving needs. Such needs can be as divergent as computer programs, new forms of energy, new methods of communication, and things we can't even imagine today.

Let me give you just one example. The FAA – the Federal Aviation Administration – has decided to commission the airlines to develop a new communications system for air traffic. This system will replace radar. It will use satellite communication to specifically locate all aircraft. It will increase air safety while, at the same time, allowing for greater air traffic. This software will be developed by a relatively small group of software engineers drawn from our major airlines....one of Robert Reich's "webs".

It is really interesting to note that the FAA did not want this new communications technology developed by means of a government contract because the procurement process is so slow, they were afraid that the technology would be outdated before their competitive bidding process selected a contractor.

Even if they don't realize it, the FAA has recognized that our economy is changing and that the old rules won't work.

Where do you go from here? Let's first remember that one of Dr. Martin Luther King's greatest lessons to us was that life is a series of choices. When faced with injustice, we must choose to fight or walk away. When faced with opportunity, we must choose to take a risk, seize the opportunity, or stay in our comfortable "industrial age" job.

God gave us a mind, a mind that can make you think positive or negative; a mind that can propel you into the new information age, or trap you in the dying industrial age. It's true that a slave who is free on paper, but doesn't know he's free or doesn't think he's free, is not free.

Remember, if you always do what you've always done, you'll always be what you've always been. We cannot wait for a fairy godmother to do things for us....we must use what we have to get what we want! You need to take action, now, more than ever before. You need to lead the way. You need invincible determination!
Action is what lifts an idea, a hope a dream off a page and gives it structure...action and action alone does it.

Folks, if I offered you a twenty dollar bill right now, to stand here and give a speech, if you're like most audiences in America, nobody would come forward and take the $20 bill. Taking Action is the number two fear in America...just after public speaking. But, it is Action that creates the winner...that's w-i-n-n-e-r, in the world of business.

Action separates the positive thinker from the dispirited; the satisfied from the frustrated; even the happy from the unhappy. Most of all, Action get things done! Action overcomes fear. We must learn to take risks if we are to succeed in business. As a great African-American once said, "one who risks nothing, has nothing, does nothing, is nothing."

Risks are studied regularly by business persons. I don't take risks in the literal sense. I measure risks and so should you. It is very unlikely that someone will surface one day and save you from the humdrum of your life or your job. You must look to yourself for your redemption and survival. You must be that incorruptible, courageous, person willing to face the status quo squarely in their face and not blink.

You must rise above the past and transcend the future...if you take the high road of sacrifice verses the low road of submittal, success is attainable. Frederic Douglas once said, "power never concedes to anything but power, never has and never will".

My question to you is..."do you have the vision to recognize opportunity in our rapidly changing economy, the courage to trust your instincts and ideas in spite of those who will work against you in defense of the status quo, and the endurance to act upon your ideas?"

Or, will you bow down to the status quo defenders, letting fear lead you to mediocrity or failure? You and only you decide who or what you will follow. Those who confess negativity with their mouth often wonder why they fail.

I believe that now, more than ever, we must, "question authority". Each of us must challenge the system which tells us we can't succeed alone; the system that tells us we must trust the status quo to lead the way, make the rules, and ref the game. Women and African-Americans in business get the same message..."take it easy, don't rock the boat."

We are the children of two great revolutions. The first was the civil rights revolution of the 1960s and 1970s. The second is now upon us. The first revolution gave us the self-confidence that only comes with complete citizenship – the right to vote, to elect our own, to influence and change public policy from the local school board to the U.S. Congress.

The second will call upon that self-confidence to give us courage in pursuit of new ideas. New business opportunities and new fortunes. If you are willing to challenge the system and be part of this change, the world will embrace you.

The classic definition of an entrepreneur is that of one who embodies the true spirit of free enterprise...she takes risks...trusts her judgment when others doubt her course...this is the true character of American business...the character of the men and women who built this country.

Conservative business leaders – quite possibly the very people for whom you work – maintain the status quo and actually stifle creativity. The executives who are not risk oriented frequently lose their job or lose your job when the company goes under, because they devoted all energies to maintaining the status quo...to protecting the old boy's network. Don't listen to them if you know you have a better idea.

Moses was not great because he found the promised land; Moses was great because he left Egypt...let us leave Egypt.

I invite and urge each of you to enter the free enterprise system. I believe in the simple things in life...you should occasionally stop and smell the money. There's nothing like the smell of dew on a newly minted $10,000 bill.

Let's leave Egypt!

Let's take Action!

Let's make the information age the historic turning point for black entrepreneurs!

Let's make the good old boy's network...the home boys network.

You know what that means.....*Mo* money! *Mo* money! *Mo* money!!!!

"The Shaping of Black Entrepreneurship in the Next Millennium...the 21st Century Awaits You"

Morehouse College Executive Lecture Series

October 29, 1997

It is my pleasure to come before you today.

As I stand here looking out upon this audience of our best and our brightest, I can think of few things more exhilarating than this opportunity to pass on to a new generation my knowledge of the world of business and my vision of black entrepreneurship in the twenty-first century.

I am proud to join the long list of distinguished leaders who participate in the *Executive Lecture Series* for the sole purpose of helping you find your own path to success—

In business, in your personal life, and in service to your community.

Thus, my mission here today is to descrbe how I perceive the world of business and discuss what qualities I believe are necessary to succeed in the twenty-first century.

I'm going to begin by sharing with you a lesson I learned from reading J.Paul Getty's biography. You may want to take notes. His four basic steps for success are:

1   Know your business better than anyone else
2   Continue to research and improve your business
    When other people are sleeping eight hours a night, you
    sleep for just six hours
3   Discover oil!

I am now, and will always be, a student of business. I have learned that the business world and the opportunities it brings are never static. . . Both are always changing. I have learned to change with it. . .To recognize emerging opportunities and seize them whenever possible.

Today, I would like to share some of my knowledge and experience with you, and discuss what I believe the future can offer to those who have the vision to recognize change and the courage to pursue their vision.

It is my belief that the American Dream is for everyone. And it's through the free enterprise system that the dream will come true. I'm certain you've all heard this before, and the lingering unanswered question is. . "How do I recognize those opportunities that will lead to success?"

I'm going to begin my answer with a short history lesson.

You've heard people say that history repeats itself. I believe this is true, but not in the way most people perceive the repetition. Let's examine our history for a moment.

Let's look back one hundred years. What do we find?

The 1860s witnessed a great change in our social conscience . . . The civil war brought emancipation, the end of slavery, and propelled the movement toward civil rights.
Individual and political freedom gained in the 1860s laid the ground work for the first American black entrepreunerial spirit that would blossom in the 1880s and grow throughout the early twentieth century.

The 1960s witnessed the re-emergence of civil rights as a movement of social conscience.

Passage of the civil rights bill and the voting rights act institutionalized our individual and political freedoms and laid the ground work for rebirth of our entrepreneurial spirit that would blossom in the late 1980s and throughout the 1990s.

The 1870s –

Reconstruction witnessed historic numbers of blacks elected to political office.

In fact, during this period, blacks comprised a majority of the lower chamber of South Carolina's state legislature. Although still physically segregated, blacks excelled in business and the professions as never before.

The 1970s –

The effects of the voting rights act are felt at every level of politics — city, state and federal with the election of blacks to Congress being the most visible and most significant to economic freedom.

The 1880s –

Individual and political freedom give birth to an entrepreneurial spirit that built banks, insurance companies, and thousands of black owned small businesses — all of whom found their economic base within the black community.

In fact, the building I own in Denver was originally the American Woodsmen's Building – one of the largest black owned insurance companies in history.

The 1880s also witnessed the emergence of the 'Robber barons', the concentration of wealth at the top, and the economic dislocation of great masses of people. Fear of sweeping economic change led to the formation of renegade 'hate' groups such as the Ku Klux Klan. America was moving from an agrarian society to an industrial society. The futurist author, Alvin Toffler, calls this period the 'second wave'.

The 1980s

Affirmative action programs in employment and business development created the catalyst that brought forth our entrepreneurial drive, rekindled that spirit of one hundred years before, and gave birth to a new breed of black entrepreneurs.

The 1890s

Right now, I'm sure many of you are straining to remember what happened in the 1890s. This period is known as the Gilded Age. The time of the "lost generation" described so eloquently by F. Scott Fitzgerald. But, it was also the decade in which America became a full fledged industrial society. The 1890s through the early 1900s was an entrepreueurs dream time.

1899: Thomas Edison built the first electric power plant in New York and John D. Rockefeller formed Standard Oil company;

1903: Henry Ford began mass production of the gas engine automobile;

1908: The model-T Ford made automobile transportation affordable for middle class Americans.

You didn't have to be a Henry Ford or a Rockefeller to prosper in this environment. The visionary entreprenuer of the 1890s-1900s would have looked at the model-T and recognized a fortune in the manufacture of tires, steel, and even piping for automobile seatcovers!!

He or she would have looked at the growing use of Edison's light bulb and the ability to distribute electric power to masses of people and recognized a fortune in the design and manufacture of lamps.

The black entrepreneurial class excelled in this period of rapid change and opportunity:

-By 1898, there were nineteen hundred black owned businesses in America; most were small retail outlets, but some were large enterprises;

-In 1900, there were 40,000 blacks in business or business related occupations; twenty years later there were over 74,000.

-Black entrepreneurs were at the forefront of the new industrial age – organizing factories for the production of mattresses, cotton goods, oil, shoe polish, and hair preparations.

-One of the greatest black entrepreneurs of that time was Madame C.J. Walker who made a fortune manufacturing and selling hair products. In 1917, she was recognized as possibly the first self-made female millionaire.

The 1990s –

The true convergence of individual, political and economic freedom — the new 'black middle class'...pervasive and firmly entrenched in American society. Black professionals at every level of business, government, and society.

What happened in the 1980s and 1990s that parallel the 1880s and 1890s?

The 'third' wave appeared. We've moved from an industrial society to an information society. At the same time, an emerging global economy has changed the rules of competition and profitability. . . American textile, automobile, electronic and oil industries find it difficult to compete in a global economy. Masses of people have been dislocated by this change, as before. Now, the renegade hate groups are called militas.

What have we learned from this brief history lesson? We've learned that we are in a comparable period of change and opportunity. The 1990s and the beginning decades of the twenty-first century are America's change from an industrial society to an information society.

This change will be most notable in the fields of communication and transportation, but it will also change our family structures, our work habits and environments, our educational system, and of course, our economy.

If we could resurrect an 1890s entrepreneur, he or she would look at this emerging information age and see countless opportunities in the distribution of information, in the development of new ways to communicate an idea and market a product. The emerging wireless communications

industry will propel these opportunities to a global scale.

And, if you think globally. . .Think about this.

- Fifty percent of the world's population has never made a telephone call;

-But, one of the most sophisticated telephone networks in the world is in Rwanda, where 100% of the main phone lines are

points when I didn't endure that I lost, the points that I continued to play that I won. Great performance requires stamina and endurance.

You must have confidence and self-esteem

Great performers have faith in their ability to succeed, confidence in their vision for the future, and trust in those they have chosen for their team. It's your confidence and self esteem that builds loyalty and trust among your team members — whether they are business partners, co-workers, or your employees.

You must learn to anticipate events

Great leaders learn to anticipate the course of events. They anticipate what is about to happen and place themselves in a position to move the event to their advantage. They examine the options a competitor has, and move in advance to control the event.

You must remain focused on results

This is perhaps one of the most difficult skills to master. Great performers don't settle for second best. If they lose a point, they don't dwell on the loss, but focus instead on winning the next point.

Our rapidly changing economic environment, the spirit of black leadership that came before you...those who laid the ground work for your progress and future success...provides an opportunity for each of you to compete at the highest levels. . . To write the rules of the game. . .If you have the vision to understand how the new game will be played.

Robert Reich, president Clinton's former Secretary of Labor, has studied this change and determined that the rules will be established within a global, not national, economy and by small groups of entrepreneurs who develop the skill and ability to: (1) recognize a need; (2) fill the need; (3) and broker their ideas or products to those who demonstrate the need.

He envisions the new global economy as comprised of large multi-national corporations and "webs" of small entrepreneurial businesses that serve their evolving needs. Such needs can be as divergent as computer programs, new forms of energy, new methods of communication, and things we can't even imagine today.

This new world of global communications and information dissemination is already destroying geographic barriers to success. It will also destroy other, more insidious barriers such as race, gender, and physical disability. It is an age when performance and results determine success....an age that begs for the kind of energy and leadership found only in the entrepreneurial class.

Where do you go from here? Let's first remember that one of Dr. Martin Luther King's greatest lessons to us was that life is a series of choices. When faced with injustice, we must choose to fight or walk away. When faced with opportunity, we must choose to take a risk and seize the opportunity, or let success pass to those who do.

Where do you go from here?

An article in the October issue of Ebony Magazine discusses the 'paradox of black/white America'. The first paradox is that everything has changed, yet nothing has changed. This means we have not yet reached the bottom line — the integration of money, power, and resources.

The second paradox, growing out of the first is that black America is one of the richest countries in the world with a total annual income of $324 billion dollars. But, this fortune flows out of the black community, not within it. Thus, the paradox of the poor rich country.

Poor yet making many rich, weak yet making many strong. Black America holds in its hands unfocused riches and the power of numbers that will determine the fate of our urban centers.

On the eve of the twenty-first century, black America is a complex paradox of opportunity and despair. With an annual income greater than India, Switzerland, and Sweden, black America cannot find the resources to bring their brothers and sisters out of poverty, provide inner city children with a quality education, health care and hope for the future.

As stated in the Ebony article, 'black America...is a symphony of contradictions in search of a theme and creative conductors.'

I'd like to close by leaving you with this challenge: I'm going to give you three facts about the future—actually three enormous opportunities. I challenge you, as a group of our best and our brightest, to employ the elements of great performance I've discussed this evening, create your own versions of Robert Reich's webs, and describe how you, as a black entrepreneur, will shape the twenty-first century and, in doing so, eliminate the paradox of the poor rich country.

The three facts are:

1   For the next 10 years, someone in the U.S. Will turn 50